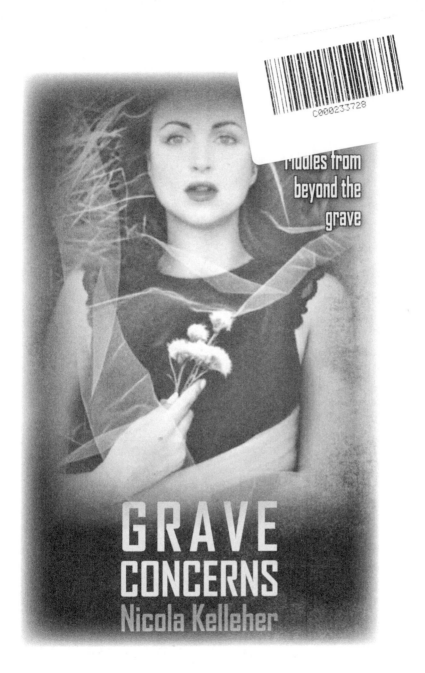

riddles from
beyond the
grave

C000233728

GRAVE
CONCERNS
Nicola Kelleher

SunRise

SunRise

First published in Great Britain in 2022 by SunRise

SunRise Publishing Ltd
124 City Road
London EC1V 2NX

ISBN 978-1-9144892-9-7

Copyright © Nicola Kelleher

The right of Nicola Kelleher to be identified as the author of this work has been asserted by him in accordance with the Copyright, Designs and Patents Act 1988.

All rights reserved. No part of this publication may be reproduced, stored in or introduced into a retrieval system, or transmitted, in any form, or by any means (electronic, mechanical, photocopying, recording or otherwise) without the prior written permission of the publisher. Any person who performs an unauthorised act in relation to this publication may be liable to criminal prosecution and civil claims for damages.

A CIP catalogue record for this book is available from the British Library.

Typeset in Minion Pro and Impact.

For Lee (1970–2022)

Contents

I have heard (but not believ'd) the spirits of the dead
May walk again: if such thing be, thy mother
Appeared to me last night; for ne'er was dream
So like a waking.

William Shakespeare — The Winter's Tale

1 Once a taphophile ...

Six-year-old hands trembled over tightly shut eyes, but curiosity forced me to peep through the gaps as my father — crouched over a decrepit, crumbling grave — pressed his guitar-calloused fingers into a gap in the earth. At 6 feet 2 inches and solid Irish, nothing appeared to scare him but, at that moment, I watched in horror as his hand was gripped by an invisible phantom which was slowly pulling him into the tomb. Like Gregory Peck in his scene with Audrey Hepburn in *Roman Holiday*, my father's face turned from curiosity to terror.

He completed the prank with a belly laugh to himself, clearly entertained by my ashen face. His laugh, if he chuckled for long enough, always turned into a deep chesty cough, having been a smoker since the age of seven. After coughing and hawking loudly for a few minutes, he assured me he was unharmed, that the whole thing was just a joke and then revealed the real reason why he had placed his hand into the tomb. He explained, with glee, that he had, in fact, found a treasure and showed me a small blue, rusty tin which he had retrieved from the hole. Too scared to look closely, or to care what was inside, I nodded to acknowledge the object as he probed to reveal its contents.

The rusty time capsule contained a small number of corroded sewing pins. As my father moved the pins around with his stubby fingers, in search of other treasures, I stood by and wondered about the implications of removing anything from a grave. I had watched documentaries with my father about ancient Egypt and I knew all too well the fate of the graverobbers of King Tut and other Pharos. Could the spirit of the grave be enraged by this blatant robbery? What if the spirit followed us home or hitched a ride with us back to our house when we left? Would we wake, in the middle of the night, to find the spirit of the grave hovering over our beds, demanding back their treasure? My childish mind pondered these questions as we walked through the graveyard.

This place, St Marks Church in Talbot Woods, Dorset, had become a weekly hangout for our family. My father loved history. I truly believed and I still do believe that he prefers the past to the present and future — he finds comfort there. Now that I am older, I can fully understand the consolation a person finds in yesteryear. We know what happened and so there are no surprises. 'Things were easier back then', some would say, 'less complicated.'

Each weekend, and sometimes on days or nights which 'looked spooky', we would pile into my father's sky blue, Morris Minor, and head into the woods. The drive was eerily quiet, and I insisted on lying down on the back seat, too frightened to look out of the window. My brother, Joe, always taunted me with things that he could tell frightened me, as older brothers love to do. I knew that any expression could give away my worries and this would always result in more mind-twisting from my brother. I dared not give him any more fuel as he revelled in scaring his little sister and seldom got told off for it. There were no seat belts in the Morris Minor and, with it being the mid-eighties, it was the norm in lots of cars, so I would hunker down until we were parked. Glimpsing, only occasionally, on the way to see smoky-looking clouds glide above, often around a hazy moon and the swaying tops of trees which sometimes evoked even more terror, as my immature brain made faces out of the branches and gave me a feeling of impending doom. Oh, how I longed for my father to take us somewhere else. A funfair, a zoo, or soft play, like normal families. However, it wasn't to be; apart from anything else, the 'boneyard', as he called it, was local and free.

On summer days the churchyard of St Marks seemed beautiful but, on wintery nights, it could look like something out of a horror film. Situated behind the church and next to open fields, there was no light for miles. In 1990, however, my feelings on the graveyard changed as I watched my grandfather, Paul, laid to rest in the top left-hand corner of the churchyard. Sunlight poured into the church in heavenly beams, which was apt for such a loving man. The lowering of his casket took place next to an open field — curious cattle had gathered next to the fence as if impromptu mourners. My grandfather was a keen gardener, an awesome joke teller, and a spectacular fisherman. My father had taken him, on request, in his wheelchair to see the cherry blossom in full bloom before he died. He saw beauty in flowers and plants and his garden was like a magical wonderland of exotic flowers, neat rows of vegetables, and succulent fruits that, as children, we gorged on.

My grandfather knew of his fate and, after suffering a series of strokes and battling lung cancer for many years, he passed away aged just 52. I was then only nine and I knew little of the man before my mother began caring for him during his sickness. We would visit him at his home in Ensbury Park, after school, and at weekends, when my mother helped with cooking and cleaning. He mostly sat motionless in his wheelchair as he watched the cricket with his eyes closed. With the remote control in his hand and with his chin to his chest, I could sometimes manage to wrangle the remote from his large gardener's hands, while he was dozing, in the hope of changing the channel to a cartoon or kids' programme. If I succeeded, there was a small chance I could watch a kids' show for a few minutes before he mumbled, with his eyes still closed, 'I was watching that!'

The funeral for my grandfather's passing came, and that day I discovered something about sorrow that perhaps was helpful to my nine-year-old self. I learned that everyone who loses someone exhibits different forms of grief. As I stood in the church pews, watching the shiny wooden casket move down the aisle, I imagined my lovely grandfather resting — as he did in his wheelchair — with his eyes closed, dressed smartly but unable to wake. I tried to cry, but no tears came. I witnessed my uncle, his only son, cry rivers and require assistance from his friends to even stand. I wondered if I was a bad person for not crying. I worried if I might be punished by God for not feeling or showing any emotion at the funeral. I was in church, after all. Was God watching me now?

I had never been to a funeral before, and it seemed so confusing for me. I had never seen my beloved uncle Lee cry so much. He was my favourite uncle. A gentle soul who always finds something to laugh about and, as a child, he gave me time to talk when many others wouldn't. He always listened to the most tedious of child chat. I loved him for that and do to this day. I wondered if Lee would ever be the same again, seeing him so broken after losing his father.

As I stood in the church and mumbled along to the hymns, I looked around the congregation and saw both of my siblings cry. A friend of the family placed his hand on the back of my head, and at that moment I realised that while some may cry when a person dies or is buried, some look to others for support and others are simply too shocked to say or feel anything. Grief is personal and there is no right or wrong way of dealing with it. Grief is made up of many layers intertwined with many other emotions.

As the years rolled on and the fear of visiting cemeteries

subsided, my interest in them increased. I relished finding out more about the people that had come to rest in churchyards. I began to look deeper into the meaning of the stones that had been so lovingly placed there by relatives, some long departed themselves. I learned not to be scared, but to be interested in the lives of these people who had once walked the earth. They too had dreams, thoughts and plans, ailments, issues, and regrets. They had loved, fought, worked hard, and made mistakes. Each graveyard holds secrets, treasures, and clues to the past and is a testament to the devotion and the love that we feel for one another. One gravestone in a local churchyard reads:

We shall find you in the grey summer garden,
amid the rain wet roses:
stir of wings,
and the morning hills behind you

Epitaphs like this offer the promise of a second life, a continuation of our association with each other, and a guarantee to get together once more. This long-held belief in the afterlife gives us hope and assists in dealing with and coping with the passing of a loved one. The prospect of an eternity of nothingness seldom provides any such support, yet some do take comfort in this style of grief management. Whatever the reason, we put so much effort into the ceremony of a person who has passed.

For centuries humans have taken great care in making the resting place of a loved one something special. However, with three quarters of funerals in Britain now being cremations, these carefully planned words and signs of loving allegiance are, sadly, less common than they were. Burial space is limited, yet over 140,000 people in the British Isles still choose to be buried each year. Deep cuts to local authority budgets, population density, and a continual need for more housing have forced many councils to spend less on local cemeteries and, as a result, burial plots have become scarcer and more expensive.

My eccentric hobby of visiting burial sites has led me to some improbable places over the years. The grave of Linda Martel on the island of Guernsey is a particularly memorable one. I visited her graveside in the spring of 2014, while filming a documentary on the Island. Guernsey is steeped in history and, as I delved deeper into its past, I uncovered many a spooky tale with living storytellers still willing to divulge such accounts. The grave of Linda, who was just five when she died, looked well-kept and loved, even though she perished almost sixty years ago. Her headstone is black and shiny with a small etching of the child in the top left corner. She lies in St Sampson's Churchyard, situated atop a cliff overlooking St Sampson's Harbour.

Linda was born in St Peter Port, in 1956, with an array of medical conditions including hydrocephalus and spina bifida, and she was not expected to live for long. After just eleven days in the hospital, she was moved to a hospice but, to the surprise of her doctors, she remained stubbornly alive. Over the next few weeks, the child's head grew disproportionately large due to her condition. Too poorly to be cared for at home, Linda was nursed in hospital by nuns and it was during this period that her father experienced a strange nightly phenomenon in which his room was filled with glowing light and he heard a sound like wind blowing.

Linda had benefitted from a new and somewhat experimental American treatment by which some of the fluid inside her head was drained away. The procedure was successful, and the size of her head reduced. After the operation, Linda's speech developed quickly, and she was described as mature for her age and wise beyond her years. She frequently spoke about a lady in a blue dress whom she called 'my lady' and often talked about Jesus

Christ. Despite being in the care of nuns for almost all the first three years of her life, the child had a great disdain for places of worship and members of the clergy. When clerics visited her, although normally a kindly child, she was said to speak very rudely, or abruptly to them, often refusing to see them at all. Linda's parents, Eileen and Roy, recalled how, most nights, they would hear voices when Linda was in her bed but, when they got up and went down the passage in their home to investigate, the voices simply stopped. They never fully heard what was said, but Linda would always tell them afterwards, 'My Jesus Christ has visited me.'

Linda told her mother, on several occasions, that Jesus Christ was behind her, or that she had passed him by and, as her mother had not acknowledged him, she thought that to be very rude. 'You walked right past my Jesus Christ,' Linda would say to her. 'And you did not even say good evening'. It became a common conversation between the family. However, that was not the only thing that was unusual. One day her father, Roy Martell, came home from work saying that he had a terrible migraine and needed to lie down. Linda spoke softly and said: 'I will make it all better'. She gently touched her father's forehead with her tiny hand and, within half an hour, Roy's headache had gone. He had no more migraines after that day.

Linda's healing powers didn't stop at her family members and word quickly spread across the Island. She received visitors from miles around, all hoping to receive her healing. Those who knew her would recall how the little girl would tell someone to sit down and could then detail any ailments that they might be suffering from. Each time she diagnosed a person, she proved to be correct in telling them exactly what was medically wrong with them and where the problem was. Afterwards, if agreed — and it seldom wasn't — she was said to have touched the person with her tiny hands and the illness simply went away. Linda always said, with great conviction, 'you will be all better now.' And it appears from local reports that they were!

One neighbour who benefitted from Linda's healing abilities was Edna Mahy, whose mother was very ill with asthma and had struggled with it since she was three years old. Edna knew Linda's father well and decided to take her mother to the Martel home to meet the child healer. While sitting with Linda, the child reached out her hand and touched Edna's mother on her breastbone. 'You have a bad chest,' said the little girl 'but it will be all better now', and it was. Edna recalled how her mother was often too breathless to walk anywhere but, later that same week, she climbed a steep hill in the town carrying a full basket of shopping, something she had never been able to do before. According to local legend, she never had any further issues breathing again.

Ralph O'Toole had suffered all his life with an ongoing heart complaint. No one, other than his doctors, knew the details of his condition although he suffered daily with chest pain. As soon as he walked into the room to meet Linda she said, 'you suffer with your heart.' Touching the man on the chest, he too was said to have been healed of his ailments and he later appeared on television to recount Linda's healing.

Reports say that Linda did not have to psychically touch a person to heal them, and she was able to do this remotely for those too poorly to make the journey to see her. Her family recalled how she could hold onto a photo of a person and, again, diagnose an illness from a distance. It was believed that Linda would hold a handkerchief close to her lips and speak a language that no one could understand (Eileen's mother suggested that this language could be Hebrew, but it was never confirmed). Eileen and Roy would then send these pieces of cloth by post to the person, and they too would later be healed of their illnesses.

Word soon spread beyond the Island and Eileen and

Roy were inundated with requests for the handkerchiefs. They had to purchase dozens of hankeys every week, as the requests flooded in. Linda was also said to have been able to tell if a person was dead or alive, simply from a photograph. When questioned on how she could perform her healing and predictions she would always say 'It's not me, it is my Jesus Christ'.

In the final months before her death, Linda began to recall accurate details of people who had passed away long before her, none of whom she had met or known. Eileen's father died in 1953, three years before Linda was born. When he was alive, he had only one eye and Linda had never seen a photo without a glass replacement. Eileen recalls that her father's sight was never discussed, yet she told her mother, one day, with great conviction, 'My grandpa is OK now, he can see.' When Eileen asked her daughter what she meant, Linda replied 'He has two eyes now'.

The irony of this story is that While Linda was able to heal many in her short life, she was sadly unable to use that gift to heal her own diseased body. As time ran out for Guernsey's miracle child, she continued to devote her time to healing others. Long before her death in the winter of 1961, Linda predicted her own passing. She told her mother, in her final days, that Jesus would not be coming again. 'My Jesus Christ isn't coming any more, I am going to visit him.' Within three months of her prediction, and after experiencing considerable body pain, Linda finally passed away. The requests for her healing, however, did not stop at her death and Eileen and Roy continued to send small squares of Linda's clothes all over the world, right up until the day when they too passed away.

Since her death, Linda's grave has become a place of reflection and comfort for those in need. Visitors often place flowers and toys on the grave for her, and some bring pieces of cloth to absorb her healing powers or place photos of people who are sick, in the hope that her powers transmute beyond the grave.

The last known case of Linda's miraculous touch was the story of a woman from Northumberland who had received one of these small squares. She had suffered from bone cancer since the early 1970s and, in 2010, received a small square of white cloth from a friend which had been cut from one of Linda's dresses. She later claimed, in a national newspaper, that her cancer had been cured by the child. Could it be possible that Linda was still working miracles from beyond the grave? Are these stories simply the product of autosuggestion and positive thought? Whatever the reason for Linda's amazing abilities, it is clear that there will always be visits to her grave and she will for ever be remembered as Guernsey's Miracle Child.

The grave of Linda Martel, Guernsey's Miracle Child.

2 Vampires and satanic rituals

Monuments honouring the rich and noble dominate cemeteries across the globe. These gravestones, usually elaborate, often attract tombstone tourists like me. Perhaps some of the most spectacular examples of funerary design can be found in London's Highgate Cemetery. Commissioned and built in 1839 as part of a campaign to alleviate overcrowding in existing parish burial grounds, Highgate quickly became a necropolis for the wealthy. Every corner of the graveyard is choked with invasive vines, overhanging trees, lovingly carved epitaphs and intricate stonework.

In the eastern corner lies the burial place of Karl Marx and his family. Marking what is, arguably, the world's most famous tomb is an enormous, larger than life, bronze sculpture set on a marble platform. Creeping ivy sneaks around the pedestal which overwhelms the area, leaving the other gravestones to pale in comparison. Funded by The Communist Party of Great Britain in 1956 and designed by Lawrence Bradshaw, the monument replaced a less formal grave for Marx and involved the exhumation and reburial of many of his family members including that of his wife, Jenny, who passed away just fifteen months before the author of *Das Kapital*.

Marxism remains, for many, the most influential political idea of modern history. The memorial still receives daily visitors and Marx remains as controversial in death as he was in life. In 2019, the tomb was attacked by a hammer-wielding vandal and daubed with red paint. The damage was repaired, but the culprit remained at large. Politics aside, the Marx family burial place is a staggering illustration of funerary engineering. It stands amid many unusual, yet beautifully crafted gravestones, but is unmistakably majestic and imposing.

Highgate remains one of the most spectacular burial grounds in Britain, perhaps, in the world: a Victorian necropolis of beautiful masonry and carefully planned architecture. There are graves that are simple and there are those that are expertly elaborate. Christina Georgina Rossetti and her brother, the poet Dante Gabriel, are buried within the cemetery walls and a desperate story surrounds them. In 1862 Christina wrote this unsentimental verse about death:

When I am dead, my dearest,
Sing no sad songs for me;
Plant thou no roses at my head,
Nor shady cypress tree:
Be the green grass above me
With showers and dewdrops wet:
And if thou wilt, remember,
And if thou wilt, forget.
I shall not see the shadows,
I shall not feel the rain;
I shall not hear the nightingale
Sing on as if in pain:
And dreaming through the twilight
That doth not rise nor set,
Haply I may remember,
And haply may forget.

Dante, overcome with sadness at his sister's passing, had written a book of sonnets which he had buried with her. Many years after her burial, at the urging of his friends and in desperate need of some cash, he uncovered her grave and disturbed the body to retrieve the book. The manuscript, however, had become entangled within the hair of his sister's corpse. It is believed that he had to hack it away from the matted tresses, before cleaning it and selling it on for a much-needed sum. He published the sonnets in 1870, in the volume *Poems by D. G. Rossetti*. The book immediately caused a scandal and was attacked as a work from the 'fleshly school of poetry'. The poems were, for the day, considered to be shockingly erotic and sensual. One, in particular, *Nuptial Sleep*, caused outrage by describing a couple falling asleep after sex.

Highgate Cemetery abounds with unusual graves, stories and legends. It isn't surprising that it attracts thousands of visitors each year and has become a tourist hotspot. Meandering through its grounds reveals a perpetual stock of astonishing Victorian and Gothic commemoration plaques. Sunken, lichen-shrouded tombstones, creeping vines, judgemental looking alabaster holy messengers, and curved trees cause the memorial park to look and feel like a scene from a Hammer movie, or the backdrop for a Gothic thriller. Small wonder, therefore, that legends surround the cemetery and, in the late 1960s and 1970s, there were reports of apparitions, even of vampires!

In 1967 two teenagers walking along the northern part of the graveyard saw a tall man in a grey coat and black top hat. They followed him for some distance before he vanished into a stone wall. Over the next decade more and more people reported sightings of a similar figure. Many said that they felt hypnotised by him, unable to move away before he vanished. It wasn't until the early 1970s, however, that events within the cemetery took a more sinister turn. There were reports of dead creatures being found in Highgate, appearing to have been exhausted of their blood, with deep puncture wounds to their necks. As sightings of the man in the top hat escalated, local Wiccan, David

Farrant, wrote to a Highgate newspaper with an eyewitness report of the apparition. He claimed that he, too, had seen a tall man, gliding above the ground, dressed in a long grey overcoat and black top hat with glowing red eyes. He was sure that the apparition was supernatural and, before long, more locals wrote to newspapers with reports of the same figure.

Sean Manchester, another Wiccan, self-described exorcist, and bishop of an unknown church, dismissed Farrant's opinions and asserted that this was, in fact, a vampire. He went on to claim that the man in grey was a King Vampire who had been resurrected by a modern Satanist and re-buried within the grounds of the cemetery. A media frenzy followed, and the press were soon reporting a bitter animosity between the two men.

Farrant and Manchester were interviewed by journalists across the country and newspaper reports continued to stoke the fires of the legend. After one especially worrying report, shown on ITV on 13th March 1970, angry locals took matters into their own hands and a mob congregated in the cemetery grounds. They had planned to hunt the 'beast' and rid the area of the supposed vampire once and for all.

Clambering over the cemetery walls in the dead of night, they broke into tombs and actually mutilated corpses, some of which had wooden stakes driven into their decaying chests. A few corpses were removed from the cemetery altogether and began turning up in strange places, leading to even wilder tales in the media. One Highgate resident discovered that, overnight, a decomposed, headless body had been propped behind the steering wheel of his car! Considerable damage was done that night, and during subsequent vampire hunts. The cemetery fell into a state of disrepair and vandalised headstones were left unrepaired. Some said that these outrages were further enraging the ghost.

Farrant and Manchester continued their feud in newspaper reports and television interviews. In a bid to settle their differences, posters began to appear all over the London Underground of a planned duel between the two men which would take place on Parliament Hill on 13 February 1973! Despite the publicity, the duel never took place. Manchester continued his press campaign to diminish the reputation of his rival and it appeared to have worked. Farrant was arrested in 1974, having been apprehended within the cemetery walls armed with a crucifix, a wooden stake, and a small bottle of holy water. Later that year, the *News of The World* published an article claiming that Farrant was a cat murderer and staunch Satanist, blaming him for a spate of cat deaths in the area. Farrant was successful in suing the paper (once, the most popular in the English-speaking world) but failed to clear his name or his reputation. He remained an oddball and charlatan in the eyes of many until he died in 2019. Manchester went on to claim to be the one who had finally captured and killed the vampire at a property in Crouch End. However, this did not put an end to the sightings, and they continue, even to this day.

In 1996, a female black cabbie claimed she almost picked up the ghost at the main gate to the cemetery. While driving her cab at night, along Swains Lane, the vehicle mysteriously began to slow from thirty miles per hour to around five. As she continued along the road, the vehicle continued to resist. Eventually, she reached the main gate and, as she mounted a speed hump, her headlights shone on a man, dressed in a long dark coat and an Abraham Lincoln-style hat. With his hand, he silently beckoned her to pull over, and she did so. But, while exiting the cab to open the door for her fare, she felt such a sense of unease that she clambered back in and drove off at speed. Looking in her rear-view mirror, she could still see the bemused man standing by the gate. She claims that she took her eye off the man for only a split second, to navigate the dimly lit road, and when she looked back, he had disappeared. A quick Google Maps search of the area shows that the walls of the cemetery, all along Swains Lane, are too high for any mortal to climb and the only opening is a gate which has been locked, at night, for decades. Could these sightings simply be the product of widespread panic? Vampire films have been popular since the late 1920s and still draw audiences to this day. The movie, *Taste the Blood of Dracula*, featuring Christopher Lee, was shot in Highgate in 1968, but this was a whole year after the first sighting by the teens.

My close friend and founder of the North London Paranormal Investigations (NLPI), Mickey Gocool, agrees with Farrant that the ghostly figure is not a vampire. Mickey and I have worked together on many ghost investigations, mostly for fun but a few for television show pilots. He is as thorough as an army general, and I trust his word. He isn't as hungry as I am to capture a ghost although, like me, he always hopes to see one, or, even better, capture evidence of one. I am always the person seeking out the spiritual reason for something on one of our hunts, whereas Mickey is often the one who quickly debunks things with his logical brain and high-tech equipment. We have caught many things on film or audio that we cannot explain but I do tend to get a little overexcited. Mickey had previously told me, on one of our phantom chasing trips, that he had seen the apparition in Highgate but, on further pressing, he refused to talk about it.

I recently reminded him of this encounter and asked if he would agree to discuss it further and, to my surprise, he did. I met him for coffee, just around the corner from the cemetery, on a cripplingly hot June afternoon. We exchanged pleasantries and discussed the foibles of the pandemic before I cut straight to the chase. 'Have you seen it then, Mickey?' I asked enthusiastically. 'It isn't a vampire, is it?' Does it match the other descriptions?' Mickey slowly sipped his coffee, and calmly began to tell me about his encounter with the so-called Highgate Vampire. He is a softly spoken man and single father of two beautiful little girls. There is a fatherly energy about him, and he is poised and gentle as he speaks — like a kind uncle who offers the voice of reason when the parents have all but given up. He was a close friend of David Farrant, during his lifetime, and talks with a quiver in his throat when speaking about the Wiccan ghost hunter.

Mickey told me, over coffee, how he and two ladies, one of whom is a psychic medium, came face-to-face with the apparition, late one night, in the burial ground. In the summer of 2012, they decided to visit Highgate Cemetery where the psychic hoped she might witness the ghost for herself. The trio arrived at the main gate at around dusk, bringing no special equipment with them, apart from their mobile phones. They stood talking for a few minutes before the psychic loudly confessed how much she hoped they would see the apparition. At that moment a man, whom Mickey described as, 'solid as you or I', appeared in front of them, apparently arriving from nowhere. There was no drop in temperature, no strange eerie feeling. The man was simply absent from the group one moment and very much present the next. Mickey went on to tell me that the strangest thing, apart from his sudden appearance, was an unmistakable odour of spoiled eggs. It smelled, Mickey said, like the sulphuric acid and iron fillings, mixed in a chemistry experiment, he had remembered from his school days. Like the apparition, the scent seemed to come from nowhere.

The man they saw closely fitted the descriptions recorded in decades of sightings. He was tall and wore a stovepipe hat, with a long dark coat and Victorian-style clothing. The group stood for a while in complete shock before wondering if the whole meeting had been an elaborate setup. The man looked very real, and Mickey wondered if he were simply a prankster, dressed up as part of a very macabre, but quite marvellous joke. Nonetheless, Mickey told me that what happened next has never been discussed, written about, or even talked about amongst the group since. He asked the man a series of questions. He replied in a confident, refined English accent which, Mickey recalled, sounded rather like the actor, Nigel Havers. When asked, 'Are you the Highgate Vampire?' he replied, 'Of course not, I have been mistaken for many a man of stature.'

During the conversation, Mickey claimed that the spirit had supplied locals with bodies from the cemetery, during his time as caretaker, for a price, with no questions asked. He remained tight-lipped when repeatedly asked his name but did give the group one final piece of fascinating information. When asked, why he was here? the man explained 'I worked in Lincolns Inn Fields before my father passed away, and then I took over his role as caretaker of this cemetery, in 1813, when I ceased to work in a legal capacity'. After these words, Mickey said he became unfocused on the man, who simply vanished into thin air. Mickey admitted that he was annoyed with himself for letting his guard down and allowing the spirit to slip away.

The group did not record the meeting but did make a voice note of the encounter, for future reference, on their phones. There are previous reports of people claiming to have encountered the spirit, who said that they felt hypnotised by it. Could this have also happened to my friend? Was the taxi driver who encountered the spirit, in 1996, also hypnotised into thinking her taxicab was driving slowly? Mickey told me that he had never seen anything like this in his life. He also explained that it frightened him more than anything he had ever witnessed. He confessed that the two women were scared stiff and, at the time, Mickey wanted, as any fatherly figure would, to protect them in some way and be the one who stayed

24

calm. On the inside, however, he admitted that he was shaking in his boots.

The medium still refuses to talk about the experience but told Mickey that the spirit followed her home and left her drained and depressed for months. The spirit, Mickey thought, had left deep scars on the whole group. I have known Mickey for over ten years, and I had asked countless times for him to tell me what happened that night in Highgate. After the conversation, I could hardly believe what I had heard.

The account sounded farfetched, yet Mickey had nothing to prove. He wasn't trying to sell his story or trying to pitch a TV show idea to me. I felt honoured that he was prepared to share it with me. Later, Mickey told me that he had always wondered if the information given by the spirit that night, checked out and was sceptical over the timing it had given. Highgate was commissioned to be built in the late 1830s, but the spirit said he became caretaker there in 1813. I dashed home to my computer and searched the Internet. After trawling through several websites, I discovered that there were, in fact, burials taking place in that same spot, although possibly on a much smaller scale, as far back as 1793. My mind raced as I poured over old documents, searching desperately online for a name of a person who had worked at the cemetery in the early 1800s. If I could find a man's name, and another's whose surname matched, it might be possible to validate the story. However, what was even more exciting than this, I concluded, was that if my research could prove that the spirit was real and that Mickey had indeed had a real time conversation with the man, then I could be certain to be able to prove that there is, indeed, life after death!

During our epic coffee conversation, Mickey had also told me about a house in Crouch End, known as the Dracula House, due to the basement being used for satanic rituals in the 1970s. I was so excited by his account of the Highgate ghost, I had failed to listen carefully to this extra tale, yet, when using Google Maps to pinpoint the cemetery for my subsequent research, I saw that the house is located quite close to the burial ground. Mickey had told me that David Farrant used this house often although, out of respect for his late friend, he failed to tell me exactly what he used it for. Sean Manchester was said to have captured the spirit in a property in Crouch End and I wondered if it could have been the Dracula House. The building still stands, despite being gutted by fire a few years back. There have been many newspaper articles written about it, and Mickey tells me that the satanic basement is locked behind an iron gate but remains as it was when last used, with a pentagram carved into the wooden floor. Whatever happened there, if Farrant and Manchester did frequent the property, it's unlikely that they went there for just tea and scones.

It isn't surprising that Highgate Cemetery has often been featured in films, TV shows, and the printed press. It is even listed on Google Maps as a 'haunted cemetery' and it's a magnet for phantom trackers, antiquarians, and Goths. The uncanny gravestones, sinister architecture, and continuing rumours, make me certain that the legend of the Highgate Vampire will never simply vanish into thin air.

London's Highgate Cemetery.

3 Cheating death

We have all heard the phrase, 'when it's your time to go, it's your time to go'. It is, of course, true that the only real guarantee in life, is death. However, there are countless stories of people around the world for whom the grim reaper came knocking before their time had come. Whether surviving a terrible accident or just having luck on their side in unfortunate situations, some blessed people have managed to escape death, and a few have managed to do so more than once. One lady who seemed to have a busy guardian angel, was Violet Jessop, an ocean liner stewardess who managed to cheat death not once, but four times in her life.

Born in Argentina, in 1887, to Irish parents, Violet was the eldest daughter of nine children and one of only six of who survived. Child mortality rates in the late 1800s were extremely high and Victorian children led very different lives to those of today. Survival was a daily struggle for many Victorian families and oftentimes young children were forced into work, much of which was dangerous, so that the family could be fed and clothed. While today it is widely accepted that the United Kingdom has a serious childhood obesity problem, Victorian children were often seriously malnourished, sickly, and underweight. The bellies of children at the turn of the century burned with hunger daily, disease was rife and personal hygiene was often absent. Households seldom had baths, let alone hot running water and families often lived in damp, filthy and cramped accommodation, commonly lodging with many other families in wracking poverty. Without access to basic facilities, such as hot water, soap and clean clothes, people were often only able to afford to clean their face, armpits, and crotch. Consequently, infection rates for a myriad of diseases were extremely high. Toilet paper, a simple product we take for granted in the modern age, wasn't invented until around 1870, and Victorians used old newspapers and discarded corn cobs to keep clean.

Violet Jessop was born just a decade before Queen Victoria died but, for many children, life remained as harsh then as it had been at the beginning of her reign. When Violet contracted childhood tuberculosis, doctors quickly predicted that her illness would be fatal. Often referred to in history as consumption, TB, as it has been abbreviated to, was seldom something an adult recovered from, let alone a small child like Violet. The virus was so rife in the 1880s that it was reported to have killed one in every seven people in Europe. Trying to fight infection when the body is weak and half-starved, seldom bodes well for recovery. Nonetheless, Violet proved the doctors wrong and survived the disease, making a full recovery within a matter of months.

This brush with death was Violet's first but it would not be her last. She was the eldest child in the Jessop family, and when her parents became ill, she took over the care of her siblings, a commonplace event in the 1800s. Sadly, Violet's father, William, died when she was just sixteen years old and, as her mother's health was also deteriorating, Violet knew that she would have to take over as the family breadwinner. The family moved from Argentina to England, where she took up her mother's former occupation by working as a stewardess on an ocean liner. It was in this role that Violet would cheat death an incredible three more times.

She was a beautiful woman with striking, good looks. Her fair Irish skin, sparkling blue eyes, and long, thick, auburn hair turned many heads; so much so, that she was ordered by company bosses to play down her looks, as her new employers feared she would cause a distraction amongst the passengers. With her long, flowing locks tied back, and a floor length, dowdy, brown outfit to complete her look, Violet started work for Royal Mail Lines on their liner *Orinoco*. She worked hard and, after a few years of service, was able to move to the White Star Line, then considered to be the most prestigious shipping line in the world. It was here that Violet found herself working aboard White Star's lead ship — the spectacular RMS *Olympic* — then the largest ocean liner in the world and one of a new class of so-called 'Superliners'. In 1911 the launch of the gigantic new superliner attracted more than ten thousand spectators and huge media interest. It was during *Olympic*'s fifth voyage, however, that Violet encountered her second brush with death.

The *Olympic* had just sailed for New York on 20 September 1911, when she collided with the Royal Navy cruiser, HMS *Hawke*, in the Solent, just off the coast of the Isle of White. *Hawke* tore two holes in the side of *Olympic* — one above the waterline and one just below it — while suffering extensive damage to her bow. Despite the seriousness of the collision, both ships managed to limp back to port without any fatalities, but the event was a financial disaster for White Star Line, who had to borrow parts from *Olympic*'s sister ship — still under construction — delaying her completion by many weeks. The new liner, which gave up so many of her parts for hasty repairs to *Olympic*, was the second of three Olympic class liners to be built in Belfast by Harland and Wolff. When complete, she would be the largest ship in the word and would be named

Titanic after her gargantuan proportions and apparently unsinkable design.

White Star Line was then fighting a desperate battle with their arch-rivals, Cunard, to dominate the world's most profitable and prestigious route: the North Atlantic. Cunard had recently launched *Lusitania* and *Mauretania* — the fastest passenger ships then in service. White Star had opted to compete on size rather than speed and their new *Olympic* class liners would be larger than anything that had gone before as well as being the last word in comfort and luxury.

When finally completed in 1912, *Titanic* was the largest man-made object ever to have been built. It was on this ship that Violet, once again, would cheat death. According to Violet's memoirs, which were published in 1997, she had previously told her colleagues — before taking up work on *Olympic* — that she did not want to work for White Star Line: she didn't like the idea of sailing the North Atlantic because of the frequent and violent storms, and she had heard stories about the excessive demands of White Star Line passengers. Despite her concerns, she found herself on *Titanic*'s maiden voyage, sailing from Southampton on the 10th of April 1912, along with almost three and a half thousand others.

On the evening of the 10th of April 1912, in the rush to get the much-delayed vessel to sea, reports claim that an ancient maritime tradition was ignored, and no bottle was broken across *Titanic*'s bow. She set sail to a fanfare of cheers and media attention but, just four days later, disaster struck, and Violet found herself at the centre of the most notorious maritime disaster in history. Hitting an iceberg just before midnight on 14 April 1912, Violet was fortunate to be one of the few on-board *Titanic* who was given a place on one of the scarce lifeboats.

The temperature of the sea that fateful night was said to have been around -2.7 Celsius, which is cold enough to cause hypothermia and subsequent death for those immersed for more than half an hour. Crew members enforced a 'women and children first' rule amongst the passengers to avoid a stampede. Some passengers panicked and jumped into the sea with their cork filled lifejackets, hoping for salvation, but it arrived too late. *Titanic*'s sister ship, RMS *Olympic* was sailing 500 miles away when *Titanic* began to list, too far to reach her in time.

It was claimed that *Titanic*'s captain, Edward John Smith, had been heard to say, 'Even God himself couldn't sink this ship.' Despite several warnings to install more lifeboats, just 30 were placed onboard; barely half of what would have been required to take all the passengers and crew to safety. So confident were White Star Line in their massive ship, that they ignored the warnings and *Titanic* will always be remembered as one of the worst transport disasters in history.

In her memoirs, Violet recalls that as the lifeboat was being lowered into the freezing Atlantic ocean, an officer, still aboard the sinking ship, thrust a crying baby into her arms. The whereabouts of the mother were unknown, and it was too late for Violet to object, so the young stewardess soothed the crying infant and took care of the child all night. The passengers who had been lucky enough to board lifeboats were eventually picked up by the Cunard liner, RMS *Carpathia*, which navigated the ice fields to arrive two hours after *Titanic* had sunk and rescued 705 survivors. When finally back on dry land, Violet recollected how a hysterical young woman came running up to her and snatched the child away before sprinting off without so much as a thank you.

You might think that this third brush with death would have sent the brave stewardess running back to shore for good, but this plucky seafarer was not willing to hang up her uniform yet. Violet continued to work as a stewardess and, once again, managed to survive against the odds. Four years after the infamous sinking of the Titanic she was working aboard RMS *Britannic*, serving as a stewardess for the British Red Cross. Known as the younger sister of *Titanic*, RMS *Britannic*, was used as a hospital ship during the First World War when she hit an underwater sea-mine and sank in just fifty-five minutes. Jessop was, once again, able to make her way onto one of the ship's lifeboats. Having already survived two disasters at sea, she must have found herself fully prepared for what was about to happen. However, this time events were entirely different for the brave stewardess, as Violet had to abandon the lifeboat when the propeller of the sinking liner began sucking boats towards its turning blades as it descended into the icy ocean. Violet found herself swimming for her life and suffered a severe injury when the revolving blades of the ship's propeller skimmed her head. Ignoring medical attention once back on dry land, the fearless stewardess only sought the help of a doctor after a series of very painful headaches. After a full examination, the doctor declared that she had suffered a fractured skull. He also announced that her injuries could have been much worse, had it not been for the lucky stewardesses' thick main of hair. Not surprisingly, Violet became affectionately known in social circles as 'Miss Unsinkable' but, despite being almost killed in these three marine disasters, she continued to work for White Star Line (which later merged with Cunard) until she retired in 1950. After a brief marriage to a man accused of being a bigamist, Violet Jessop moved to a small cottage in Suffolk where she lived out her years and kept chickens. She never remarried and finally died of heart failure at the age of eighty-three. Her headstone lies in Hartest Cemetery in Suffolk.

The story of Margorie McCall which dates from around 1705, is so steeped in folklore, it is hard to tell which parts of it are factual. However, her gravestone, which is located in Shankill Cemetery, Lurgan, Belfast, Northern Ireland, reads:

Margorie McCall
lived once, buried twice

Such an epitaph is enough to have any would be grave hunter running to the nearest library for more information. Shankill Cemetery, surrounded by homes and established trees, is easy to miss if you don't know it's there. Once discovered, its wrought iron gates and grey brutalist headstones are enough to send a shiver down the spine of the bravest. There are no weeping cherubs to comfort you here; just row after row of stone slabs, all of a similar style and shape. The cemetery dates from around 1690 and many of those who are buried here were the workmen and women who helped to build the town but have long since been laid to rest. It began life as a double ring fort — commonplace for burials in the Bronze Age — and the outline can still be seen today. Those who visit this place get a sense of the ancient past, intermingled with a few contemporary headstones. It's a hotchpotch of broken stones, sunken ground, and vandalised masonry. The tomb of Margorie McCall seems not to have been spared when vandals ran amok. It is split and faded yet appears to have been restored — perhaps by a family member determined not to let the hoodlums erase her memory. The headstone now sits encased within an iron frame. Other unloved monuments lay shattered and fragmented around it.

Margorie was married to a doctor, John McCall, and they lived with their children in Church Lane, Lurgan, a short walk from the cemetery. Theirs was said to have been a happy life but the 1700s were hard, and famine was just one of the issues they faced. Disease, a by-product of the ongoing famine of the time, was rife and many ailments that today could easily be treated, were then fatal. It is said that Margorie fell ill and suffered a raging fever which caused her husband to fear for his wife's life. The fever worsened until Margorie finally slipped away in her sleep.

The family held a wake, as was the tradition, but concerns were raised about the valuable wedding ring that Margorie was wearing, and her husband thought it would be wise to remove it. However, even after several family members attempted to remove the ring, it was clear that it would not budge. The recently deceased body had swollen during her bout of infection and the wedding ring had to be interred with her.

She was buried quickly, in Shankill, to avoid the spread of disease. However, news travels fast, especially in a small town like Lurgan, and whispers of a recently deceased Doctor's wife buried with a small amount of gold was enough to prick the ears of local thieves. Grave robbery was rife in the 1700s and lookout towers were set up in many cemeteries to avoid the exhumation of corpses, which were often sold on the black market to medical students for their studies. Lurgan, however, had no such security at the time of Margorie's passing and it wasn't long before thieves unearthed her body.

The grave robbers, now faced with the same issue as the family members, decided to hack the wedding ring from Margorie's hand in a crude and hurried grave-side removal, using an unknown mechanical tool. But, when cutting into the skin of the fourth finger of Margorie's left hand, blood spurted from the wound and Margorie abruptly sat up, opened her eyes wide, and loudly wailed like a banshee, then clambered out of the vault, blood dripping from her hand.

The grave robbers ran for their lives while Margorie simply brushed the earth from her clothing and walked back to her home near the cemetery. Her husband, distraught with grief, was sitting at the kitchen table with his children, making a final toast to his wife, when he heard a familiar knock on the back door. He said to his children, 'If your mother were still alive, I'd swear that was her knock.' When he opened the door he saw his wife standing in front of him, still dressed in her burial clothes and covered in earth, with blood dripping from her hand. He is said to have dropped to the floor in shock.

Some reports say that John McCall's hair turned white overnight and others say he died right there, in front of his recently resurrected wife. Whatever the finer details were, the legend of Margorie McCall continues to be something that the townsfolk of Lurgan talk about, even to this day. Despite a few unconfirmed facts and many more Chinese whispers, it is clear that this woman was a real person, and her headstone substantiates at least part of the tale.

It wasn't until the late 1800's that autopsies became commonplace, so it is unlikely that any thorough tests would have been performed on Margorie when she seemingly slipped away, after a fever, the first time. Even though she had a doctor for a husband and despite sleeping through a funeral, family wake, and a subsequent burial, it was clear that Margorie McCall, on that night in 1705, was simply not dead when she was admitted to the ground. Following her recovery, Margorie went on to enjoy a full life, and some locals recall how she even went on to re-marry and give birth to several more children, before finally passing away some years later. It is also believed that her husband, John, is buried in the same plot that Margorie had climbed out of the night the robbers tried to surgically remove the ring from her finger.

There are further murmurs amongst townsfolk that go on to claim that, when Margorie passed away on an unreported date, she was pregnant by an unknown suitor. Local historians who have tried to reveal the authenticity of Margorie's 'lived once, buried twice' epitaph are said to have spoken to many living relatives of previous Lurgan residents, who confirm the legend in various ways. These include a surviving relative of the local policeman whose job it was to guard the cemetery in the late 1800's. Although likely not present when the woman's first or second death took place, the policeman had told relatives and friends that he believed the tale to be entirely true and saw no reason why it wasn't so. In Lurgan, the legend of the woman who lived once but was buried twice, will continue to be talked about for centuries.

Another man who was not so lucky in cheating death was John Sutton, a naval lieutenant, whose almost completely eroded gravestone can be found, half-sunken, in St Mary's Church Cemetery, in Cowes, on the Isle of White. Sutton was a passenger on a ship called *Grace*, which had anchored outside Cowes on its way to South America. Sutton was a well-educated man and the nephew of Lord Thomas Cochrane, 10th Earl of Dundonald: a British naval officer and a radical politician. Cochrane had previously led several successful missions during the Napoleonic Wars but was described by many as a mercenary and was dismissed from the Royal Navy in 1832 over an alleged fraud involving the stock exchange. He was later reinstated after a pardon and, when he died in 1860, held the rank of Admiral.

It is believed that his nephew, John Sutton, may have joined the Royal Navy with a personal desire to emulate his uncle's great adventures, but his journey to stardom came to a halt one night in Cowes after a round of heavy drinking. He picked a fight with the wrong man and refused, several times, to bury the hatchet.

Sutton was just 22 years old when he came ashore and went for a few drinks with some of his shipmates at the Dolphin Inn, in Cowes, where many other passengers from the *Grace*, were also enjoying a few nightcaps. Sutton was already quite inebriated when he arrived at the inn, nevertheless, the drinking continued and as the evening ramped up, he joined a game of billiards, placing a stake on the winner, which was a large amount of wine. An evening of raucous laughter and vulgar jokes ensued, but the loud and obscene commentary from Sutton and his crewmates began to irk the other patrons of the bar.

Sutton started to joke about the other passengers' true reason for their journey to South America; claiming that everyone on board the *Grace* was probably setting sail to escape debt. An army major called Orlando Lockyer, who was also drunk, took immediate exception and demanded an apology. Sutton tried to defuse the argument by claiming that all men were, in fact, in debt to God. but that was not enough for Lockyer who challenged Sutton to a duel, before taking a tender back to the *Grace*, to retrieve his pistols.

The ship's captain warned Sutton, via a handwritten note, which was passed to him back at The Dolphin Inn, but the young lieutenant ignored him and continued to drink. It was reported that he could be seen stumbling around the streets of Cowes and was heard bellowing sea shanties, well into the early hours of the morning. Lockyer had been to bed but even in the cold light of day, neither man was prepared to back down.

The next morning Sutton and Lockyer met, with a surgeon and two seconds, in a field near Northwood House, the home of the Ward Family. Sutton had no intention of either firing or apologising, but Lockyer was determined to duel. The surgeon set about measuring the distance between the two men, as was customary, and each man was handed a loaded pistol. Lockyer fired first and Sutton stepped forward, extending his hand in an apparent apology. Lockyer had extended his own hand in acceptance, but it was too late. The bullet from Lockyer's gun had struck Sutton between the third and fourth rib, piercing his heart and killing him. He dropped to the ground and, when the surgeon confirmed that nothing could be done for him, the remaining men fled.

Lockyer was arrested at a Portsmouth inn a few weeks

later and the other men shortly afterwards. At the Coroner's inquest, the jury returned a verdict of 'Wilful Murder against Lockyer' and all the men were tried for murder at the Winchester Assizes. If found guilty, they would have hanged, but the jury could only agree to the lesser verdict of manslaughter, and they were each sentenced to just three months in prison. The Ward family, who owned the estate where the fatal duel took place, were said to have been horrified that such an act was committed on their land. John Sutton was laid to rest in the nearby cemetery. His headstone reads: 'To the memory of John Sutton, who fell in a duel near this town on 10 December 1817 aged 22 years.'

4 Any old iron

Burial space has been in short supply for centuries. When my grandfather died in 1995, his son, my uncle Lee, was persuaded by the chaplain to opt for a double depth grave plot, ensuring that his own final resting place would be secure when he passed away. Aged just 19 when his father passed, I recall my mother telling me that my uncle had paid a premium for this option. It appeared from conversations that I had managed to secretly listen to (while pretending to play alongside my family members at my grandfather's funeral) that my uncle was lucky to have been offered such an opportunity. These extra-deep grave plots were very much in demand and becoming scarce. Cremation was not available until the 1880s and did not become popular until the 1960s. The need for many to secure a burial plot is the reason we have so many vast and intricate cemeteries around the country today.

In the 19th century, England's population skyrocketed and by 1825, its capital city, London, was the largest in the world. With a population of close to two million, burial space was not just a need for the bulging city, it was a necessity. British MPs, impressed by the notable cemetery in Père Lachaise Paris, France, commissioned the building of the so-called Magnificent Seven. These beautifully laid out cemeteries were designed to offer a place of contemplation for families and secure plots for future generations if a family could afford it. The main reasoning, however, was to alleviate overcrowding in smaller parish cemeteries which, at the time, were filled close to capacity. In fact, overfilled churchyards were so compacted with corpses that human remains had begun to seep into the city's water supply, causing epidemics of diseases including typhoid and cholera. Building new cemeteries within the city was, therefore, seen as the answer to a London-wide public health emergency.

The first of the Magnificent Seven to be built was Kensal Green, which was completed in 1833. Originally called The Cemetery of All Souls, it is still in use today and my grandparents, who emigrated from Ireland and settled in Paddington in the 1950s, are buried there. West Norwood cemetery was completed in 1837; Highgate in 1839 with Abney, Brompton, and Nunhead all completed by 1840. The final cemetery to be commissioned and built was Tower Hamlets, which opened in 1941. This cemetery resides in the East End of London and was originally known as, The City Of London Cemetery but is known locally as Bow Cemetery. It was quickly filled to capacity after its completion and ceased to operate as a working cemetery in 1966.

The East End was heavily bombed in World War Two, due to its proximity to the docks, and Bow Cemetery was not spared, being bombed five times during the Blitz and left unrepaired for decades. The cemetery has, however, recently undergone a much-needed makeover. It's a stone's throw from where I have lived since moving to London from Bournemouth in 2005, and where my partner, Bradley, grew up. Bradley has told me countless times how, as a child, he and his friends would dare one another to run through the cemetery at night. It was open 24 hours a day for many years and remains so. Bradley was a tough little boy, born and bred in the East End, but he told me how he would genuinely feel terrified when it was he who had lost a bet and whose forfeit it was to make the spooky dash through the graveyard. He even recalls how, later in life, he would sometimes use the cemetery as a shortcut when making his way back home from a local nightclub called Benjy's. Too drunk to take a long walk home to his parent's house in Devon's Road, he would hastily walk through the cemetery, with much the same feeling as he had endured during the childhood games of dare.

He recalls how the grounds were poorly maintained, if at all. 'The whole cemetery was pitch black at night and many of the graves were so badly damaged, or sunken, that if you slipped in the wrong place, it was possible to end up in a deep hole. The grounds were also heavily overgrown with weeds and the whole area was infested with rats; a far cry from how it looks today.' The restored cemetery is now listed as a nature reserve, much to the delight of the local rodent population, and volunteers maintain the site as an area of conservation and education. A team of helpers regularly updates visitors via standing chalkboards with bird sightings and lists of butterfly species that can be witnessed, fluttering about the grounds.

Bow Cemetery might not have as many stars to spot within its grounds as its West London counterparts, but it certainly makes for an interesting walk and discussion. Built in one of London's poorest areas, frugality is the theme here, as many of those buried here had little money for a funeral or burial. In some areas of the cemetery, up to forty people are buried together in what are known as pauper's graves.

Funerals have always been a tremendous expense for families and, at the turn of the century, those who couldn't afford to pay for a good send-off would be placed in an unmarked grave — usually with other recently deceased people — financed by a local charity. These low-cost burials often included workhouse occupants, beggars, and those who simply couldn't be identified. With no family to mourn and no headstone or tomb to mark the burial site, this type of final resting place was something that many Londoners feared. London councils still have *Bono Vacantia* offices, who try and locate the relatives of those who have died alone. In cases where no next of kin can be found, the council arranges and pays for a funeral. The 2014 movie *Still life* depicts a council officer who goes further than his managers expect to try and give such people dignified funerals. Sadly, he is often the only mourner to attend.

Early deaths were commonplace in the mid-1800s when Bow Cemetery was completed, mostly due to the spread of disease through unsanitary living conditions and a contaminated water supply. The passing of loved ones was so frequent and heart-breaking, that families began to plan more elaborate and ritualized mourning. The trend for extravagant funerals was fuelled by Queen Victoria who, when Prince Albert died of typhoid fever on 14th December 1861, spent the rest of her life in mourning, wearing black for decades and refusing to be seen in public.

Funerals in the 1800s became status symbols. Ostentatious burials, elaborate tombs, and overdone funeral processions were commonplace for those who could afford it. The idea of 'doing things properly' following a bereavement became so important for Victorian families that households at the lower end of the socio-economic scale would often sacrifice food and clothing to pay for their children's funerals. Child mortality rates were high across the United Kingdom, but forfeiting nutrition, clothing, and even shelter to pay for a child's death often brought it about sooner.

Funeral clubs began to pop up all over the British Isles, which involved paying a weekly sum into an account organised and held by committee members. A large, lump-sum was paid out on the passing of a child, regardless of how long a family had held their membership. Sadly, these clubs soon fell victim to swindlers, who would join several clubs and, in the event of a child's death, would claim several amounts for one death. There were even accusations that some merciless parents resorted to murdering their children to claim a funeral fund, only to have them buried in a pauper's grave, which had a considerable stigma in Victorian times. Nevertheless, Bow Cemetery is the final resting place for thousands of paupers whose families simply could not afford to bury them in the way that they would, almost certainly, have preferred.

Bow Cemetery is close to London's docks and sailors who died at sea were also often buried there in pauper's graves. In 1871, 29 men who drowned in the Thames were buried together after *Princess Alice*, a wooden pleasure steamer, collided with another ship and sank. The disaster, which took place by Galleons Reach, claimed more than 700 lives in total. Originally built in Greenock, Scotland, *Princess Alice* was purchased by The London Steamboat Company in 1867 and was used to carry passengers along the Thames for day trips to Sheerness and other destinations along the Kent Coast.

The City of London was filthy then and the constantly expanding population made for highly unsanitary conditions, resulting in a constant battle against disease. Day-trippers seeking to escape the toxic smog, faeces-caked streets, and nauseating stench of the city — particularly in the height of summer — crammed into paddle boats like *Princess Alice* simply to breath some much needed fresh air. Captained by William R H Grinstead, the SS *Princess Alice* was originally called *Bute*, but when she was sold to The London Steamboat Company, they decided to change her name to *Princess Alice*, after the third child of Queen Victoria.

Mariners have a superstition that when a ship is complete and has been formally named, the name goes into the 'Ledger of the Deep' kept by the sea gods Neptune and Poseidon. Renaming a ship or boat is thought to bring bad luck: it can infer that you are trying to slip something past the gods, and they will punish your deviousness. However, if an owner does decide to change the name of a vessel, many sailors consider it necessary to perform a re-naming ritual, usually breaking a bottle on her hull. This ritual is said to prove to the sea gods that you have no deceitful motives. Whether this ancient rite was performed for SS *Princess Alice* or not, her story ended in tragedy.

On 3 September 1878, while returning from Sheerness jam-packed with passengers and crew, almost all onboard died when she collided with another ship, *Bywell Castle*, while passing Galleons Reach. After breaking into three pieces, she sank within minutes. Horrifyingly, in the days leading up to the incident, approximately 75 million gallons of raw sewage had been disposed of directly into the River Thames, at the exact point of the disaster. A headcount had not been taken and with captain and crew all dead, the exact number of fatalities will never be known.

Captain Grinstead had most likely not followed the correct path and it soon became clear that between 600 and 700 passengers and crew had drowned together in the filthy, effluent-filled waters of the Thames. 130 survivors were pulled from the river that night, but many had ingested the polluted water and succumbed to a slow and painful death sometime later. A memorial to the Captain and all who perished can be found in Woolwich Cemetery. The remaining 29 crew are buried in a pauper's grave.

Placing a large volume of rotting corpses into one place was not without its issues in the nineteenth century. One account, recorded in 1838, tells of an incident involving a pauper's grave that resulted in the death of two London men. Thomas Oakes was a well-seasoned grave digger, aged around 53 years and he had been ordered by the sexton of the parish of St Botolph in Aldgate, to dig exceptionally deep graves for the ever-growing numbers of deceased paupers. He was also told to only cast earth on top of a coffin if disease were the cause of death. Bodies were often stacked on top of one another with little or no material in between. Many of the coffins were of poor quality having been provided by charities who relied on donations to purchase them. These simple, low-grade boxes were often made of cheap wood and crudely assembled, resulting in a rapid decay of both box and corpse. Decaying bodies housed in poorly made, rotting coffins balanced on top of one another, invariably caused problems. The stench from oversubscribed paupers' graves was a significant nuisance in Victorian London. St Botolph's jam-packed cemetery had been reported countless times to officials, but nothing was done.

One morning in 1838, Thomas Oakes was busy trying to excavate a grave plot even further. Oakes had been asked, by the sexton, to ring the churchyard bell at around 10.30 am that morning as he had been taken ill and could not perform this daily task himself. However, when he did not hear the timely chime, he asked his daughter Mary to go down to the Churchyard and investigate. It was there that she found Oakes lying dead in the deeply dug, open grave.

A crowd gathered, and a young man named Edward Luddett offered to retrieve Oakes in the hope that he might be revived. On entering the grave via a wooden ladder, witnesses reported that Luddett acted as if 'struck by a cannon'. Stunned, he stopped dead in his tracks and fell backward into the grave next to Oakes. Unknown to the crowd, Luddett had also died.

Held up by ropes and a team of willing volunteers, William Thomas King — who had proceeded Thomas Oakes in the role of gravedigger — gallantly tried to retrieve the two bodies. But, on entering the grave he reported feeling faint and was lifted back out of the hole to recover. He also reported that the flame of a candle he was holding had mysteriously extinguished. He was sure that the deeply dug hole and the presence of so many rotting corpses had created a deadly, noxious gas that had caused the two men's deaths. Rotting corpses produce carbonic acid gas which, when inhaled, can cause instant death. It is also now used in fire training to extinguish flames. Thomas Oakes and the brave Edward Luddett didn't stand a chance against the poisonous vapor. Their bodies were eventually retrieved and the practice of digging such large graves finally came to an end.

One of the things that strikes you as you wander around the grounds of Bow Cemetery — apart from the abundance of tall, unkempt grasses, overhanging trees and fragmented pathways — is the number of monuments featuring a stone urn. Always expertly carved to appear as if draped in fabric, these monoliths are everywhere. Many of the headstones have succumbed to decades of British weather and, sadly, the names of those to which they belong have long been expunged.

The trend for this type of monument was commonplace in Victorian England and most of the grave plots that hold them appear to be from that time. The urns — almost always shaped like the classic funeral urns used to hold cremation ashes — symbolise the return of the physical body to dust while portraying the soul as everlasting. This type of headstone has links to pagan traditions as, in years gone by, ashes from cremations were commonly collected and buried in an old or roughly made cooking pot. Over time the containers became more elaborate but modern cremation urns are not dissimilar from the ones seen in Victorian times.

The urns we see today on grave monuments are often styled on ancient Roman and Greek designs. The carved stone fabric represents the veil between the two worlds: that of the living and that of the dead. It is said that the world of the living and the spirit world overlap, but are separated by a thin layer, often referred to as 'the veil'. It is also believed that, at certain times of the year, especially Samhain or Halloween, the veil becomes thinner and the lines of communication between the two worlds are stronger. The appearance of these draped urns in a cemetery, however, usually depicts the veil between life and death and the crossing of one plane to another.

Another common tombstone style found in almost all cemeteries is the broken column. I first saw one of these as a child as I walked around St Marks Cemetery with my father on one of our family outings. St Marks, which opened in 1870, is still a working cemetery and when I first saw a broken column in its grounds, I innocently thought that it had been vandalised. The column, which had been recently carved and was made of pure white alabaster, was too fresh to have been damaged by pollution or eroded by the weather. I asked my father if we should report the broken stone to the Vicar, whom we knew quite well. My father explained that it was a new stone, and it was supposed to look that way. I learned that day that this particular monolith often commemorates someone who died at a young age, or in their prime.

Walking around the grounds of Bow Cemetery, and seeing similarly shaped monuments again, made me wonder what the prime of life for a person was, or is. The average life expectancy for a person living in London today is around 80 years of age. However, in the East End, which is still, for the most part, home to many on low incomes, the life expectancy is staggeringly lower at around 56 years for women and 60 for men. Statistics such as this give you a real sense of your mortality.

I visited this cemetery with my partner, Bradley, and we are aged 39 and 42 respectively. Tombstones like these — monuments representing people of our own ages — started to put a lot into perspective for us. Many of these graves were centuries old and life expectancy a few hundred years ago was vastly lower than it is now. In Victorian London, the life expectancy of a labourer, for example, was just 19. The thought of lying six feet underground without having lived out our years sent a shiver down our spines.

Large monuments, imposing tombstones, and beautifully worded epitaphs are often a final gesture to a loved one whom you simply didn't spend enough time with. One of the most prominent tombs in Bow Cemetery is the Westwood memorial. Joseph Westwood was an engineer, boilermaker, and shipbuilder. His company quickly grew, and he became owner and partner to several engineering companies around the East End. Eventually, he joined forces with another engineer, Robert Ballie, and the two began working from an ironworks on the Isle of Dogs. It is clear from the sheer scale of Westwood's final resting place — it features a Grade 2 listed spire that has been expertly carved out of Portland stone — that he did well for himself and his family. His imposing tomb overshadows nearby monuments.

Westwood had nine children and his wife and eldest son, also named Joseph, continued the iron trade well into the early 1900s. It is rumoured that West Ham United was born from a football team set up by the workers employed by Westwood and Ballie at the ironworks, thus giving the legendary team their nicknames 'The Hammers' and 'The Irons'. Westwood passed away in 1883 and West Ham United was founded in 1895. Nonetheless, it is possible that a team of ironworkers, enjoying a friendly game of football during downtime at work, were the beginning of the legendary, East London team.

The East End is famous for its jovial cockney characters who are often portrayed in books and films. The local accent has been mimicked and mocked for centuries. Dick Van Dyke's portrayal of a jolly chimney sweep in the Disney film *Mary Poppins*, cemented the 'cockney character' in minds and hearts across the world. To any real cockney, his accent was far from accurate but, the idea that a person residing in the East End of London could perhaps offer a kind ear, an upbeat joke and perhaps a tinkle on an old piano, wasn't too far from the truth.

One well known and much-loved Tower Hamlets resident in the late 1800's was known as The King of Limehouse. In 1932, the funeral of Charlie Brown, a publican from Poplar, attracted a staggering 16,000 mourners. Charlie had no regal connections or upper-class family members. He was simply a man who was loved by all those who knew him, and many did.

He was the owner and proprietor of the Railway Tavern, which stood at number 116, West India Dock Road. A former boxer and sailor, Charlie Brown became something of a local legend. So much so that his pub became known locally as Charlie Brown's. Tending to thirsty sailors who rested ashore while their ship's cargo was being processed at the nearby docks, he was said to have exchanged beer and other beverages for the trinkets and objet-d'art offered by the sailors and travellers who had exhausted their cash from excessive drinking or other onshore-pursuits. He became famous across the world for his hospitality and generosity. He was so loved that he became friends with cabinet ministers, sailors, journalists, and anyone who had the time to lend them his ear.

As his list of friends grew, so too did the collection of curios which he proudly displayed in his pub. He was reputed to own treasures including Ming vases, Louis XVI cabinets, Waterford crystal, and a large collection of silver, gold, and ivory. Among the array of priceless items, however, he also had a less valuable collection which he kept in a room below the bar. Here he displayed the objects mainly brought in and traded with sailors. These included a stuffed two-headed calf which also had six legs, along with stuffed seagulls, snakes, and alligators. He also was said to have had a collection of jars filled with formaldehyde containing small mammals or fish. Horrifyingly, one of these jars was said to hold the body of a badly deformed stillborn baby.

Outside of his peculiar collection, Charlie was mainly known for his kind words, open heart, and the epic nights held in his legendary pub. The piano would play almost constantly at Charlie Brown's, and people would dance and cheer all night long. It was a happy place to forget your troubles and, if you couldn't afford a drink, there was always a deal that could be struck with Charlie. He was physically fit and powerful with a busted nose from his boxing days, and they said he could quash a brawl with just one look, ensuring everyone involved made up and went back to having a good time.

So loved by his neighbours was Charlie, that both he and his vast collection of expensive antiques always remained secure, despite living in one of the most crime-ridden areas of London. His death, in 1932, sent shockwaves across the East End and made headlines around the world. He kept the secrets of those who would trust him, and he was honest, ungrudging, and generous. When 16,000 people descended on Bow Cemetery to pay their respects to the much loved face of the East End, police were drafted in to keep order, but no one stepped out of line that day.

The curios were divided between his children and the pub was run by his daughter Ethel until it was demolished in 1989, to make way for the Docklands Light Railway. A new hotel is currently being built on the site of the old pub, but there is still a plaque where Charlie Brown's pub stood. Locals who grew up long after Charlie had passed still speak with great affection of him, his pub and his vast collection of nick-nacks. When he was buried in Bow Cemetery, street hawkers sold memorial cards outside a graveyard packed with people and covered in floral tributes. Some still say that a part of the East End died the day that Charlie Brown departed this world, and it will never be the same again.

It is not easy to navigate your way around Bow Cemetery, but the volunteer team which helps to run it has planted herbs and non-native flowers. In one spot there is an overwhelming scent of the oregano which grows freely amongst other plants and herbs. Bins have been placed along the footpaths, but some areas of the cemetery still appear impenetrable, not least due to the exceptionally tall grass, crumbling headstones, and the sheer volume of graves which, in some places, are almost stacked shoulder to shoulder.

Practically every inch of ground in this cemetery holds the final resting place of at least one departed soul (if not several) and the contrast between rich and poor is evident everywhere. As you explore you know that you are, almost certainly, treading on the final resting place of many a poor Londoner for whom there is no longer any visible monument.

Customers in Charlie Brown's celebrated Limehouse
pub, the Railway Tavern.

5 Pirates and murder

One of the first gravestones to pique my interest when I moved to the East End in 2006, was one that I stumbled across while walking my long departed, miniature English Bull Terrier, Oscar, through the churchyard of St George-in-the-East. At the time, I lived a few roads away from the church and it was a great place for walking a dog as it is a quiet churchyard, walled off from the local area. English bull terriers have a lot of energy and aren't huge fans of meeting up with other dogs, so Oscar and I used to play fetch alone until one of us, usually me, became tired and we made the short walk home.

The intriguing grave that I came upon one snowy November morning was one which I later learned is known to locals as the 'Pirate Gravestone', and it is the resting place of Alex Wylie, who passed away on 5 December 1741. His headstone features a skull and crossbones design along with the inscription *Memento Mori*. It lies with many others, stacked against the churchyard wall like soldiers on parade.

The Wyllie grave, as it is known to church volunteers, stands out from the other stones not least because of its unusual design, but also because, unlike the other stones which are heavily covered in lichen, this one appears to be covered in bright green algae. The skull and crossbones design was a popular motif in funerary masonry in the late 16th Century, but what is really intriguing is that the Wyllie grave also features the word 'Sacred' at the top of the stone and has an inscription that begins 'Here lieth'. It is otherwise not overly different from other headstones of its age, but it is the only one in this cemetery with this particular appearance. I challenge anyone, stumbling across this grave, not to stop and stare. It seems bizarrely out of place, even for a graveyard that dates back to 1729.

When I first discovered this fascinating stone, my curiosity got the better of me and I began to use the Internet to search for clues. I found lots of references to the inscription *Memento Mori* including modern stones with the same inscription. The phrase is Latin and translates to 'remember you must die'. It is a reminder, that death is not the final frontier but an open door to a new world; some might say: the next chapter in life. The Internet is a wonderful source of information, but it only took me so far. What I also found was that many visitors to the churchyard had been just as inquisitive as me and the Internet was awash with photos of the gravestone. Most, like me, had thought that Wylie, having been buried a stone's throw from London's docks, must have been a pirate! Had he been captured at sea and brought back to Britain to be hanged? It is not such a farfetched idea. In 1701, the pirate Captain Kidd had been executed for piracy in nearby Wapping where permanent gallows were maintained especially for pirates. Kidd was actually hanged twice. On the first attempt, the hangman's rope broke and he survived. Although some in the crowd called for Kidd's release, claiming the breaking of the rope was a sign from God, Kidd was hanged again minutes later, and died. As a final humiliation his body was gibbeted over the River Thames at Tilbury Point — as a warning to future would-be pirates — for three years. Was the phrase, *Memento Mori*, a reminder that he knew that he might ultimately face justice, and so lived each day as if it were his last? I yearned to know more about this man and his gravestone, so I set about finding someone who might know.

I started first with an online ancestry website, which amounted to almost nothing. I tried various spellings of the Wyllie surname but alas, I found nothing of interest. I began to think outside the box and look at the facts that I had. I was so deep in taphophile heaven at this point, I felt it was my duty to clear Alex Wyllie of his piracy crimes or, even better, prove he had committed some. This headstone, in my over-excited mind, had all the makings of a Johnny Depp movie character.

I dug deeper and deeper into the past I just had to find out more. I had to find out who Mr Wyllie was and why he had such an awesome-looking gravestone. Every minute I had to spare was devoted to searching for him online, looking through records, speaking to parish volunteers, and pouring over crumbling paper archives. I longed to find a story of a mischievous sea-faring man, who had looted the seas and had found himself ashore on London's docks. Documents and archives seldom hold real dates and correct spellings and are often written in ink and difficult to transcribe. I met many dead ends as I found church records had been lost, spellings of Wyllie, had changed several times within archives and I began to lose all hope of finding the story behind the pirate grave. However, one last search and a fresh set of eyes from one of the church volunteers meant that I was able to finally match the man with the skull and crossbones headstone and found out his story after all.

Alex Wyllie was not a pirate. He was born in Scotland and went on to marry a lady in Derbyshire. It isn't known how he ended up in London, but I now know from records that his headstone was made in the North and carved out of sandstone, in a bass relief setting, then sent to London by sea. The green algae covering that I was so intrigued by appears to be very common in headstones made from sandstone. It was then normal for young men to leave a family behind and set out to make their fortune. It is not known what Mr Wyllie did, but I found no record of criminal activity, or time at sea. I did, however, find a record of his mother, Elizabeth Templetoun.

When I searched further in the archives, I found that the name Wylie is connected to the Knights Templar and that graves depicting a skull and crossbones often have a masonic link. In Scotland, his homeland, headstones featuring a skull and crossbones were commonplace and are simply a reminder that we must all, one day, die. The explanation seems to be simply that Wylie commissioned a traditional, Scottish style memorial to be lovingly carved and sent to London for his burial.

Skulls on headstones are often depicted smiling and are simply a reminder that when a person leaves this world they pass to a better place where those they are leaving behind will, at some point in the future, be able to join them. The skull and crossbones emblem is not limited to Scotland or the UK and appears on memorials all over the world. However, because Wyllie's gravestone is the only one remaining in St George-in-the-East with this dramatic motif, it looks starkly different from the others.

The older headstones that remain in the churchyard of St George-in-the-East once stood next to many others but, at some point, graves were cleared, bones removed and a few of the more important memorials were chosen to line the outer wall. Why the Wyllie stone was among them remains a mystery but, perhaps even at the time of his burial in 1741, the stone was already unusual.

My strange and unusual hobby grips me like a psychological thriller and forces me to look back into the past, searching for clues. It's like a treasure hunt for the truth — one that keeps you up at night, thinking about possible links to the past and ways of proving them. Not far from Wyllie's headstone is that of the Williamson family, who were victims of one of London's most notorious murderers.

The churchyard of St George-in-the-East is located along a road called The Highway, which dates back to Saxon times and was, at one point in history, known as The Ratcliff Highway. The name Ratcliff was borrowed from the word Red-Cliff and refers to the red sandstone cliffs the road was originally carved through. In its infancy, the road extended from Wapping Marshes right down to the South of London. St George-in-the-East was designed by Nicholas Hawksmoor and was set to become one of fifty churches commissioned after the coronation of Queen Anne in 1702. The ambitious building plan was intended to help secure a Protestant succession and each church was purposefully planned to tower over the homes of the working class as a stark reminder of religious reform.

The East End then had a growing population of immigrants, many of whom had arrived via the nearby docks and few of whom were Protestants, never mind Anglicans. Dedicating the church to St George would serve as a reminder to any foreigner of the primacy of the Church of England. The outer walls of St George-in-the-East were understated in comparison to many European churches but, once you are through its large wooden doors, the interior of the church looks and feels less austere. The church was consecrated in July 1729, one of just twelve of the fifty planned churches that were actually completed. Originally Parliament had proposed that the building of the churches be funded by a tax on coal. However, the elaborate designs, huge material costs, and need for a large workforce, resulted in plans to build further places of worship to be abandoned.

St George-in-the-East still stands proudly along The Highway and the recent development of the site has created a more peaceful and reflective environment for visitors. Ancient mulberry trees surround the church and manicured lawns — as well as a children's play area — give a more welcoming air than Hawksmoor may have originally intended. Parliament had intended to promote strict reforms in the area when the church was built. The Highway, which lies adjacent to London's docks was, and still is, situated in one of the poorest boroughs of London. When the church was completed in 1729, the surrounding area was almost semi-rural, with open fields and poorly built homes. As the area was developed it became popular with sailors, foreign traders, bootleggers, beggars, and prostitutes and it acquired a fierce reputation for violence and crime. In December 1811 the neighbourhood became notorious as the location of a series of grisly killings, known as The Ratcliff Highway Murders. Two, separate, brutal attacks were made on the Marr and Williamson families, just twelve days apart and shockwaves were sent across London.

The first of the attacks occurred late one night at 29 Ratcliff Highway, which was also a linen shop. Resident Timothy Marr, who was also the shop's proprietor, was closing up and decided to send his maid, Margaret Jewel, out to purchase some oysters for supper; a family treat for his wife Celia who was recovering from the recent birth of her son, Timothy, in a back room of the store. The baby was 14 weeks old and sleeping soundly in his crib in another room shortly before midnight when Margaret left to run her errand. On finding several fishmongers closed, she returned to the shop empty-handed. When she arrived at the store, she found that the doors were locked, but the shutters appeared unpinned, which was unusual. She knocked on the door but failed to raise her master from his quarters.

At that moment she heard unusual noises coming from the shop and also heard little Timothy crying a low cry before she heard a thump and then total silence.

Alarmed, she backed away from the storefront and alerted a local night watchman called George Olney. He knew the Marrs well and knocked on the door, calling out to the shopkeepers. The noise had awoken another local man, John Murray, a pawnbroker who was the family's next-door neighbour. Murray decided to climb the back wall of 29 Ratcliffe Highway and investigate. Finding the back door wide open, and the shutters unlocked, he gingerly entered the building via the open door.

Murray's blood ran cold as he witnessed a horrific scene. Laid out in front of him was the mutilated body of the shop's young apprentice, a boy called James Gowan. He was lying by the bottom of the stairs in the store, in a huge pool of blood. The boy's face had been smashed in and his brains were strewn about the walls and the floor. There was a large amount of blood splattered across the counters of the shop and the neatly stacked linen he had been folding that day. It was total carnage, but the misery didn't end there, in fact, it had only just begun.

Holding a handkerchief to his mouth to withhold the urge to vomit, he called out to Olney. As the nightwatchman entered the house he found Murray, ashen faced, transfixed and completely petrified with fear as he stood, in the dim light of a candle, next to the body of Celia Marr. She too was lying face down on the floor, blood still pouring from her battered skull. It was as well that Murrey knew her, as it was difficult to identify the corpse: every inch of the poor woman's head, had been brutally pulverized. Murray, still reeling from shock, called out into the street, to raise the alarm. 'Murder, murder!' he shouted to the crowd that was gathering, 'Come and see what murder is here!' A few minutes later they found the body of Master Marr who had suffered the same fate. Battered beyond recognition, he lay behind the shop's counter drenched in blood and splattered with brain matter.

Margaret Jewell, overcome with grief, was now

screaming outside the store. The horror of the scene, and the realisation that she had cheated death by minutes due to her long and fruitless errand, sent her into severe shock. It was then that another neighbour called out in the crowd, 'What about the baby?' The crowd waited in silence hoping to see Olney or Murray, emerge from the store with news that the young child's life had been spared, but it wasn't to be. The killer had spared no one in the little linen shop. Onley and Murray confirmed that the child too had been murdered and was lying dead in his crib. The poor infant's face had been crushed almost completely on the left side and his throat had been slit with such force that his tiny head was almost severed and separated from his body.

The commotion in the street brought more neighbours to congregate outside the shop and the Bow Street Runners (London's first paid policemen) soon arrived on the scene. A search of the premises revealed that, oddly, nothing had been removed from the property and all of the day's takings were still in the till. There appeared to have been no motive for the murders, but an assumption soon spread that the maid, Margaret, had arrived before the killer was finished. She had heard the baby cry which indicates that she may have scared off the killer before he could loot the building. There were some who thought that the murders might be due to a revenge attack on the Marrs: an unhappy customer perhaps, or a person who may have owed the Marrs money.

Whatever the motive for the violence, it created fear amongst the shopkeepers of the East End with many closing early in the weeks that followed and some refusing to stay open at all. As Christmas approached, however, shopkeepers had no option but to reopen their stores and extend the hours to pay for the festivities and the subsequent downturn in trade that always occurred in the New Year. As the story began to fade and hope began to build that this terrible attack was just a one-off, a similar attack, just twelve days later, would have the area's locals reeling with fear once more.

On the night of 19 December the publican, John Williamson, his wife, Elizabeth, and their barmaid, Bridget Harrington, were closing their pub, the Kings Tavern on New Gravel Lane, when the killer struck again. Witnesses saw the Williamsons' lodger, John Turner, scrambling, half-naked via knotted sheets, from the upper floors of the pub. A patrolling night watchman was called to investigate as Turner was heard shouting that a murder was being committed within the house. Several men joined the night watchman and were able to force open the cellar flap to the pub and begin a rapid search.

They were horrified to discover the body of John Williamson hanging from a ladder in the cellar and the bodies of his wife Elizabeth and barmaid, Bridget Harrington in the kitchen area. All three had been brutally battered to death. Their throats had also been cut in what appeared to be a carbon copy of the recent atrocities involving the Marrs. There were further similarities to the Marr murders in the supposed method of escape too, which appeared to have been across open land at the rear of the premises. Only one person (other than Turner) survived the attack. Kitty Stillwell, the Williamsons' fourteen-year-old granddaughter, had slept through the awful incident and thus had luckily evaded being found by the murderer.

The second murder caused widespread outrage amongst the locals and newspapers ran lurid headlines, striking fear into the hearts of locals. 'Horrid Murders' read the headline from the *Sussex Advertiser*. 'Another Most Dreadful Murder' ran the headline of *The Star*. For the next two weeks, the killings were the sole topic of conversation across the East End. Terrified residents hid in their homes, shopkeepers once again closed early and took on extra apprentices for security. A wooden ripping chisel, known as a maul, was found by police at the Marrs' shop on the night of the murders. It had been overlooked by the first officers to arrive because a blooded shipwright's hammer had been found close to the body of Marr and was assumed to have been the murder weapon.

The wooden maul was clear of blood but, on further investigation, the object appeared somewhat out of place, and it soon became clear that it did not belong to the Marr family. Perhaps it was carried there by the murderer who had intended to use it but had dropped it on the way out of the building? Further inspection revealed the initials JP carved into it. Implements like this were valuable tools of trade and the initials would almost certainly have been those of the owner.

Many arrests were made, and hundreds of people questioned, but the murders were no closer to being solved until 24 December, when the wooden object was finally identified as belonging to a seaman named John Peterson, who resided at the Pear Tree Tavern. This information came via a man who, at the time, was incarcerated in Newgate Prison on debt avoidance charges. His name was Vermiloe and he was the landlord of the Pear Tree Tavern, in Wapping. Also lodging at the Pear Tree was a man called John Williams and Vermiloe claimed Williams had taken the maul from Peterson intending to use it in the brutal murders. There was a substantial reward for anyone information leading to the arrest of the murderers, which was certainly something a man in severe debt, such as Vermiloe, could use.

It didn't take long for investigations to result in the capture of John Williams and on 27 December 1811, he was arrested and later appeared before magistrates. The courtroom was packed, and many were already convinced that Williams was the murderer, even though the case against him rested largely on the unsubstantiated testimony of a debt-ridden criminal.

The magistrates were particularly keen to question

Williams about a torn and bloodied shirt found at his lodgings and also extra money that had been found in his possessions after the murder of the Williamsons. But, when Williams was due to arrive in the dock, a solemn-faced prison officer informed the magistrate that Williams was already dead. He had, that very morning, taken his own life by hanging himself in his cell. Following a brief discussion, the magistrates decided to go ahead and hear the evidence of the other witnesses.

By the end of the day and having heard the rest of the evidence from various witnesses, the magistrates concluded that the now deceased Williams was, indeed, the murderer and that, furthermore, he had acted alone in committing all seven murders. Any evidence that others might have been involved seems to have been pushed conveniently to one side. The magistrates stated that the public could now rest assured that the murderer was no longer a threat as he had taken his own life in prison rather than face justice.

To further allay the fears of Londoners, it was decided that the body of John Williams would be strapped to a board, placed on the back of a cart, and paraded around the streets of Wapping and Shadwell: proof that the killer was dead and no longer a threat to society. There were fears within the judicial system that the gruesome parade might cause public disorder but, when the grisly procession made its way through the streets on New Year's Eve, 1811, a crowd of 180,000 watched peacefully. The cart stopped for ten minutes in front of the King's Arms, where the coachman reportedly whipped the dead man three times across the face.

Williams was buried in an unmarked grave at the crossroads of Cable Street and Cannon Street, with a stake hammered through his heart. Suicides could not be buried in consecrated ground and the stake was meant to stop his restless soul from wandering, while the crossroads would confuse whatever evil ghost arose from the grave.

Additionally, the grave was deliberately made too small for the body, so that the murderer would feel uncomfortable, even in death. His corpse was flung into the pit without any prayer or ceremony, quicklime was added, and the crude grave was covered over.

The Crown and Dolphin pub was later built on the crossroads and, decades later when laying a gas main for the area, workmen discovered the bones of the murderer, crumpled and in a kneeling position. The skull was removed and placed behind the bar of the pub as a macabre curio and a talking point for patrons.

The Crown and Dolphin no longer sits at the crossroads. It has been replaced by a block of flats and the skull of John Williams mysteriously disappeared from the building when it was demolished. It is not known where the Williamsons were buried after the murders, but the bodies of the Marr family were interred in the grounds of St George's Church, shortly after their deaths, and a headstone remains there to this day, placed along the same outer wall as Alex Wyllie's.

Alex Wylie's 'Pirate Grave' in the churchyard wall of St George-in-the-East.

6 Witches, werewolves & zombies

With burial plots becoming something that far outstretches the pockets of most people, more and more families are choosing to have their loved ones cremated. It is now more common for families to choose to take a person's ashes home with them after a funeral cremation, or scatter them in a place of remembrance or area of fondness for the deceased. It is more difficult and expensive now to be buried beneath the ground or in a churchyard but, due to the increase in cremations, monuments to many of the UK's inhabitants may not even be considered due to lack of funds, or lack of a burial plot.

We do, of course, now have the beauty of video, as well as highly organised archives, books, literature, and photographs which makes delving into the past more accessible and serves as a modern way of remembering our loved ones. A lack of information regarding an unusual headstone often leads me to endless searches online and emails to parishioners or churchyard volunteers as I try to learn more about a person and their grave.

One stone which required a lot of my time was the grave of Meg Shelton, also listed as Mary Shelton, known locally as the Fylde Hag or the Woodplumpton Witch. Her unusual monument dates to 1705, and rests in St Anne's Churchyard in the parish of Woodplumpton, Lancashire.

Meg, it appears, was accused of being a witch but — while that wasn't uncommon in the 1700s — Meg's gravestone really does make you wonder why she was buried in consecrated ground and why her memorial is so different from all of the others.

There are several reasons why a person could have been accused of witchcraft: bearing a mole, birthmark, or slight deformity on their face or body, being outspoken, questioning religion, or growing and collecting certain herbs. I have to say, I tick all of these boxes. Witches were often blamed for events such as failure of crops, illness in livestock, and unusual weather patterns. Magical practices and the belief in them are documented throughout history, but the belief that a human being could have supernatural influence over the natural world grew during the 16th century.

Meg Shelton lived on agricultural land, alone in a small, poorly built dwelling. It is reported that she was regularly accused of being the source of many problems in her area, including a spate of crop failures, children's illnesses, sickly livestock, and stolen and missing items from local farms and shops. One farmer accused poor Meg of the theft of milk, direct from the cow's udder. He alleged that Meg had transformed herself into a goose and had carried off the milk. One farmer even reported that Meg had shapeshifted into a bag of grain in order to spy on him as he worked. He claimed that, while working on his farm one day, he felt uneasy as he mucked out his pigs, as though someone was watching him. Turning around several times to see no one but a bag of grain, he suspected that the grain was not all it appeared to be and speared it with his pitchfork. According to him the sack screamed loudly and bled from the puncture holes.

It is more likely that Meg was a harmless eccentric who was blamed for anything and everything in her village and other criminals took advantage of her reputation to escape punishment. Stealing in the 1700s was a very serious matter and could result in a lengthy prison sentence, flogging, the hacking off of one or both hands, or even death by hanging. Anyone wishing to pass the buck for stealing in Woodplumton simply blamed it on Meg, the local hag, and often got away scot-free.

Meg is reported to have died alone in her cottage after being crushed by a barrel and a crumbling stone wall. She was probably just a reclusive, unmarried woman, scraping a meagre existence on the fringes of society. Nevertheless, the story of her burial is bizarre. After her fateful and untimely death, Meg was buried in the churchyard of St Anne's, Woodplumpton, Lancashire in 1705. Locals assumed that her accidental death was the result of her making a pact with the devil in exchange for supernatural powers. They thought that the devil must have come back to claim her soul. Nevertheless, being buried in consecrated ground seems to contradict her frightening reputation as a witch or a devil worshiper.

Surely a person like Meg, widely believed to be a witch, would not be welcomed into the grounds of a church? Nevertheless, a woman named Meg Shelton is buried in the graveyard of the church of St Anne's and her grave can still be found today. What is unusual about it is that, instead of a headstone or stone carving, the grave is covered by a very large, stone boulder. A small plaque that has clearly been added many centuries after her death now appears on the side of the boulder with an inscription, and her name is listed as Mary Shelton. The reason why she has a boulder on her gravesite instead of a headstone is somewhat disturbing. It is said that when Meg died, she was buried in the churchyard in a grave without a headstone as she likely couldn't afford one. However, the very next morning the local reverend found her corpse, lying face up, above the ground, stiff as a board and covered in the morning dew.

Several attempts to re-bury the woman's body, resulted

in the same thing every time. Finally, a priest was brought in to rebury the corpse and reconsecrate the area where she rested. She was also reburied this final time, face down, so that any attempt to claw her way out, would result in the corpse digging even deeper into the earth. The large stone boulder was placed above her, it is said, to ensure that the corpse did not rise again. Once the boulder had been placed over her grave, she never escaped. But, due to the strange shape of the grave and the legend behind it, the site attracts many visitors. The boulder remains in the graveyard at Woodplumpton to this day, marked with the simple inscription:

> *The Witch's Grave. Beneath this stone lies the remains of Mary Shelton, alleged witch of Woodplumpton, buried in 1705.*

Unsurprisingly, supernatural rumours surround the gravesite to this day. Touching the boulder is supposed to cause chills or one's hairs to stand on end. Some locals maintain that the blessing, or perhaps curse, that keeps Meg bound to her grave must be periodically renewed by visitors. It is said that, whenever possible, a visitor to Meg's grave should circle the boulder and spit upon the stone. Saliva has been documented for centuries as a powerful magical substance, there are references to the power of spitting as far back as Ancient Egypt. All the same, spitting on a person's grave seems disrespectful, if not disgusting. Another somewhat frightening legend suggests that circling the grave three times while speaking Meg's name, will result in her decomposed hands, bursting through the earth grasping from below the boulder to snatch any would-be ghost hunter. The church's website, however, offers a more cheerful legend that suggests that standing on the boulder and rotating three times would result in a wish being granted.

The fear of the dead rising from their dusty graves is

a tale played out in many horror stories. Witnessing a corpse, meandering around the earth, would of course be enough to frighten anyone, and slabs placed over graves are not uncommon around the British Isles, particularly where a person was suspected of witchcraft. The blocks of stone served to put locals' minds at ease when a person accused of witchcraft was killed or died, ensuring that they could not push through the earth and come back from the dead. Scavenger animals such as foxes have been known to dig up dead animals in a food search and it has been said that they aren't too picky over which mammal they feast upon. A reasonable guess for slabs over graves would be to ensure such animals did not uncover a person in their final resting place but a story of zombie witches sounds more intriguing.

The Woodplumpton Witch was never documented to have walked above the ground; her corpse was merely found in the early mornings lying next to her grave. It is possible a large animal could have uncovered the body in its search for food. However, one similar story of a person rising from their grave is even more chilling than the story of the Woodplumpton Witch. A gravesite, known locally as the Dobbs Grave, lies on the crossroads where the parishes of Kesgrave, Foxall, Brightwell, and Martlesham meet. The Dobbs Grave is said to be that of a local shepherd named John Dobbs, who committed suicide in 1740, after losing one of his sheep and fearing the punishment of being deported to another country. Other legends suggest that this is the grave of a highwayman or gypsy who was hanged at the crossroads as a warning to others for stealing sheep. Whomsoever the grave belongs to, being buried at a crossroads has long been considered the solution for a person who killed themselves by suicide or someone who lived on the fringes of society as an outcast. It is thought that burying a person at a crossroads would confuse the spirit who might try and find their way home and perhaps try to seek revenge in some way. Crossroads have long been thought of as uneasy, transitional gaps between unclaimed areas which were vulnerable to supernatural forces and were for many years considered to be haunted grounds and meeting places for witches.

To be condemned to burial at a crossroads meant eternal purgatory. Suicide had throughout history been treated as a crime, as many people felt that death should be decided by God, not the person themselves. However, in the seventh century the Archbishop of Canterbury pardoned suicide and argued that the outcome of a person's soul should be left in the hands of God. For many Christians, however, suicide was a crime: 'the gravest temptation the Devil inflicted on Christian souls.' For centuries there would be no place in churchyards for suicide cases and these poor souls were often condemned to burial at a crossroads. Suicide remained a crime until 1823 when an Act of Parliament allowed suicides to have a private burial in a churchyard — but only at night and without a Christian service. A review of the law resulted in a new Act in 1882 allowing burial in daylight hours, but Parliament did not decriminalise suicide until 1961.

The first documented instance of a crossroads burial was in Suffolk when, in 1510, Robert Browner, the superior of Butley Priory in the county, hanged himself after defaulting on his taxes and slipping into financial ruin. His corpse was ordered to be staked through the heart and buried at a highway crossing. Known as a deviant burial, these types of interments often took place at a crossroads, not far from where the act of suicide took place. The Dobbs grave has attracted rumour and speculation for centuries but in 1936, almost 200 years after Dobbs' untimely demise, it is said that his ghost appeared before a group of drunken vandals who decided to visit the crossroads after hearing the story of the shepherd while drinking in the nearby Bell Inn.

Fuelled on alcohol and masculine bravado, the group

of men arrived at the crossroads just after midnight and decided to dig through the earth, find the tomb, and prised open the decaying casket. When they reached the corpse, they found the bones of a man with a wooden stake through his rib cage. Realising that they had uncovered something quite unusual and satisfied that the legend's rumours fitted the story, the men refilled the hole, but not before one man in the group called Reeves removed a tooth from the skull. It is said that he fashioned it into a keepsake and wore it on a watch chain for the rest of his life.

Four years after the first desecration of the Dobbs Grave, a young airman thought it would be fun to exhume the body once more, on an appropriately dark and stormy night. The young man headed to the grave alone and began to dig into the earth to reach the corpse. However, he received the fright of his life when he was chased away from the site by an angry apparition of a young man. Not deterred by these ghoulish tales another group of brave young men, in the 1960s, bit off more than they could chew when they too decided to dig up the Dobbs Grave but ran for their lives when they too were scared away by something otherworldly. Following further desecration in 1996, the local parish council entered a long-standing agreement with landowners to secure the grave's future maintenance and today it is surrounded by a decorative iron fence, to keep away morbid trophy hunters or would-be ghost-hunters. Documents and archives of the local area reveal little about the true identity of the person who rests in Dobbs' Grave, but one thing is for certain: it is never wise to try to wake the dead.

The most talked-about gravestones in any cemetery are often ones that feature a grand design, or the name of someone well known, such as an artist, politician, or member of the Royal family. Parish ground keepers often admit that those who once lived a comfortable life have the best seats, so to speak, in a cemetery or churchyard. Large, elaborate monuments often reside by the pathways of churchyards, and those who lived a humbler life are often buried in the so-called 'cheap seats' at the back and sides of a cemetery. However, even the smallest of graves found in unusual places, often hold a great story.

In the parish of North church, Berkhamsted sits a small churchyard called St Mary's. A rather unassuming gravestone sits on a small grassy mound, among others, with a simple inscription, 'Peter The Wild Boy, 1798'. The stone looks almost fake, and its inscription seems somewhat crudely carved. It is a stone that is very easy to miss if you were not aware of its somewhat famous owner, Peter, who was discovered as a feral child by peasants in a German forest They had found a very hairy boy, of unknown age, who walked on all fours, spoke no words, and had a very unusual look. He had a vast amount of body hair, with a thicker mop on his head, flared nostrils, and a deep cupid's bow in his top lip, leading many to believe that he was otherworldly. He was aggressive, unruly, and appeared to have been foraging for food in the woods. Rumours soon began to circulate of a werewolf boy found living wild. However, the child did have some suggestions of civilisation as he wore the ragged remains of a shirt collar around his neck, suggesting that he had perhaps, at one point, had a family.

News of the werewolf boy spread and caught the attention of the King. George I was German and the first of Britain's Hanoverian monarchs. The king summoned the boy who was shipped to Britain and brought to court were all were enchanted by him. It was clear that he was not a werewolf at all, just a boy who had been abandoned and had become wild. The King set about feeding and clothing him, taking him under his wing and introducing him to royal life. He was renamed Peter and lived amongst royalty at Kensington Palace, a far cry from his endless days and nights in a German forest

At first, the court loved him and was amused by his lack of grace and his somewhat disastrous attempts to learn how to live like a gentleman. He was dressed in fine clothing, drank fine wine, and dined on the best food but, despite many scholars and members of the court trying to teach the young man to speak, he never uttered a word. He also refused to sleep in a bed, instead, he would curl up every night on the floor in the corner of his chambers.

In time, the court tired of Peter and he was entrusted into the care of one Mrs Titchbourne, who was known to the Queen and who was paid £35 a year for the boy's upkeep. Mrs Titchbourne would often spend her summers at a farm owned by a close friend and yeoman, James Fenn. The farm was located in the parish of Northchurch and Peter was transferred to the farm to spend the rest of his days there. In the country, he felt free, despite not knowing any words, he found solace in nature and took comfort in the simple life, spending his days running through cornfields and feeding the farms livestock.

In the summer of 1751, Peter went missing and a desperate search ensued. When a fire broke out in the local jail, the inmates were set free and a man who spoke no words was found amongst the criminals. It soon became clear that it was Peter, and he was returned home to his master, James Fenn. An interesting artifact remains of Peter's to this day, in a local museum. It is a leather and brass collar, with a small lock, which was said to have been placed upon Peter on his return to the farm, after his incarceration. The collar reads, Peter The Wild Man, along with his address and a message: 'whoever will bring him to Mr Fenn, shall be paid for their trouble'. The collar seems brutal by our standards, but it may have stopped Peter from straying once more as he continued to live at the farm for the rest of his life. The ownership of Peter changed hands many times, firstly to Mr Fenn and, when he passed away, to Fenn's brother. When Fenn's brother passed away, Peter, who was then in his 70's, was said to have pined for his master, passing away a few days later.

A portrait of Peter still hangs in Kensington Palace and a recent study of the man's unusual looks and reports of his behaviour and lack of speech have led experts to believe that Peter was not a wild or feral man who acted this way due to his time in the forest, but rather that he was born with a rare genetic condition, only recently discovered, called Pitt-Hopkins syndrome. Children born with this condition have several features similar to Peter including, facial deformities, speech issues, poor coordination, and severe learning difficulties. They often fail to reach certain milestones and Peter may likely have been cast out, into the forest, by his parents. Flowers are often placed on the grave where he now rests but it is unlikely that these are left by relatives as Peter never married or had children.

The Grave of Meg Shelton, the 'Fylde Hag', at St Anne's Church, Woodplumpton.

7 Holy toast

Recently, while trawling through the Internet, I found a very intriguing story about an ancient churchyard close to Dorset. Having grown up in that county, I simply had to click the link. Delving a little deeper, I found the original story which was featured in several newspapers. It made the hairs on the back of my neck stand up when I saw photographs to support the eery tale. A ghostly apparition could be seen peering over the top of a gravestone. The story told of a trio of local ghost hunters who, on a whim one night, had decided to visit Boldre Church. I noted the name of the ghosthunter who had taken the snap and set about finding the man on social media.

To my surprise I easily found the owner of the photo via Facebook — a man called Amir Jardin — but what was even more surprising was that Amir and I had mutual friends! I messaged him and asked if he would he be willing to discuss his experience with me. Within a few hours Amir had messaged me back and as we chatted over the Internet, we discovered not only that we had many mutual friends, but he also grew up in Talbot Woods, the very place where my intrigue into the unusual world of taphophilia started!

Amir told me that he had always had an interest in the paranormal and that when he lived in his parents' home in Talbot Woods, he had a number of terrifying ghostly encounters. They were not only experienced by Amir, but by the whole family. These ghostly incidents were so terrifying that even today his parents, who still live in the same property, refuse to discuss what happened and have sealed off the door to Amir's old bedroom, which was the epicentre of the activity.

Issues began for Amir and his family when, late one night in 2013, Amir claims that he was pinned to the bed by an unknown entity while watching television. He recalls that just before he was pinned he felt a surge of electricity running up and down his body, a loud hissing sound in his ear, and an overriding feeling of being watched. The experience is so etched in his mind that he will never forget what happened to him and he recalled almost every detail of the incident, even the television programme he was watching: the comedy classic *Only Fools and Horses*.

As he lay on the bed he saw the bedclothes moving but there was no one there. Then he heard a hissing sound which increased to a crescendo as the feeling of an electrical current washed over him. Shortly afterward he felt as though someone was pressing their whole body against his, but there was no one there. The force of the unknown entity almost pushed Amir over — it felt as if it was trying to roll him over. Pressed into the bed, he was unable to move and as he tried to use all of his strength to resist being overtaken, he was locked in a terrifying battle for what seemed like hours but was likely just a matter of seconds.

Eventually, the entity withdrew and released its grip on Amir. He ran yelling for his parents who were sleeping in another room, and they woke to find Amir, petrified and white as a sheet, at the end of their bed. His parents were naturally sceptical, and Amir's mother agreed to swap rooms to prove that it was just a figment of his imagination, however when she experienced the same terrifying ordeal, just days later, she became convinced that the family home was haunted. Amir went on to tell me that after he and his mother experienced the same brutal paranormal attack, things did not calm down in the house, in fact, they got progressively worse. Items would be thrown around Amir's room by an unknown force, objects would go missing in the house, only to turn up in the strangest of places. The family was terrorised by the spirit for many years and even though Amir moved out of the property, the family continue to be plagued by the entity.

Amir's father locked and sealed off his old bedroom and forbade anyone in the family to discuss what happened. Amir told me that his father believes that if they refuse to give any recollection of the incident or any life to the story of the entity, it will stay away. However, Amir fears that the entity may simply be lying dormant, for now. Just one year after the horrifying ordeal in Amir's family home, he once again experienced the hissing in his ear and the energy surge as he entered the back of a friend's car for a night out. He thinks that the surge of energy is more of a warning and sign for him and may even be a sign of protection. Although shocked, Amir got back into his friend's car along with a group of others, and the driver set off down Matcham's Lane, Dorset.

What happened next will haunt Amir for the rest of his life. The driver increased the speed of the car, taking it to 80mph and when the car reached a notorious bend called 'Dead Man's Corner' the car left the road and hit a tree. No other cars were involved in the accident and Amir, who was the only passenger not wearing a seatbelt, somehow escaped unharmed. The car burst into flames killing the driver instantly and seriously injuring the other passengers, leaving only Amir unscathed. His surviving friends were taken to hospital to be treated for minor cuts and bruises, while Amir chose to walk home. The feeling that something was protecting him, hit Amir hard that evening. Tributes were left for his friend at the side of the road and police were baffled as to how the accident occurred. After this experience, and the ordeal he suffered at home, Amir admits he was adamant he needed to find out more about the paranormal and began organising his own ghost investigations with his girlfriend Amy.

Amy did not believe in ghosts at first but enjoyed spending time with Amir and acting as the logical member of the team which often included Amir's auntie Suzanne. Amir and his aunt had spoken about visiting Boldre Church for some time but hadn't got around to it. The ancient churchyard is riddled with legend and it is not too far from Bournemouth where Amy and Amir live. Bored one evening Amy suggested heading down to the graveyard when a film at the local cinema they were planning on going to appeared to be rescheduled. Suzanne had heard a rumour in her local newsagents that Boldre is the most haunted church in the UK and so Amy and Amir called upon Suzanne to join them on an impromptu visit. As they had decided to visit on the spur of the moment, the team was only armed with their phones for capturing any spooky evidence. The three headed over to the location and on the way, Suzanne filled in the others with all that she knew about the place.

They arrived at Boldre Church, around 10 pm after just over an hour of driving. Boldre church is located in the village of Boldre, New Forest and sightings of ghosts have been recorded in the area for many centuries. Boldre Church is described on Google as a 'warm and welcoming, beautiful church'. However, when Amir arrived with his girlfriend and aunt, in the dead of night, it seemed anything but. The church sits on a small mound, in a remote area of the New Forest, which is peaceful with graves neatly spread about. The tombstones look well cared for despite some dating back centuries but, unlike other overcrowded cemeteries I have visited, the churchyard holds only a handful of graves as it is situated in a lightly populated area. There is room to walk around the graves and just a handful of trees can be found growing on the land. It is still a working church and there has been a building for worship there since around 2000 BC.

As they set about walking around the crumbling graves, there appeared to be nothing unusual about the churchyard. However, it didn't take long for Amir to find something curious as just twenty minutes into their visit, he captured something strange on his camera. When Amir stopped to review his last few shots, peering out from behind one of the ageing headstones was the face of a man with a moustache, who also seemed to be wearing a black tricorn hat. Excited by the photo, he called out to Amy and Suzanne who quickly ran over. When the two women saw the photo, they were dumbfounded. Then all three heard what sounded like footsteps frantically running around in between the gravestones. Terrified that they might not be alone, the three ran for the car, their hearts in their mouths and their minds boggling.

Amy, who had never believed in ghosts, suddenly had a change of heart and, to this day, she insists it was this experience that permanently changed her mind on the paranormal. Amir and Amy now dedicate all of their free time to paranormal investigations and ghost hunts, recording all that they find using professional equipment and posting the footage on their YouTube channel. Fans of the online show tune in every time a new video is uploaded, and Amir has been asked to appear on television and radio to discuss his findings and experiences.

Since that late-night, impromptu visit to the church, Amir claims that there has been a hive of unusual activity in his new home where he lives with Amy. Despite living together but with no other housemates, both Amir and Amy have heard footsteps in the lounge, electrical devices suddenly and inexplicably start in the dead of night, and both believe that something may have followed them back from the ancient churchyard. Amy refuses to go into the flat alone now and insists on waiting for Amir to arrive back from work before they enter together. Amir, however, is safe in the knowledge that he has some form of protection surrounding him and is content to continue living in the house.

Having been saved from the fatal car accident and having been able to fight off the invisible force that night, in his childhood room, Amir feels that he can handle anything that he comes into contact with now, either at home or on a ghost hunt. Amir's photo of the man peeping out from the gravestone went viral and has appeared all over the Internet and in many newspapers and magazines. Could it be the face of a spirit? Could the ghost of the person who was laid to rest under the headstone be peering out, perhaps, from above their own grave? The Church is certainly very old and was known to have been frequented by smugglers in the 18th Century. Close to the Lymington River, the churchyard could easily be reached by smugglers coming upstream from the coast, and they are believed to have hidden contraband including brandy, tea, and tobacco, in the churchyard to be collected later.

Smuggling in the 18th century carried a heavy penalty, a person caught with contraband could face the death penalty, which was usually death by public hanging. There is a legend that surrounds the churchyard of Boldre Church, which suggests that a corrupt judge haunts the local area having been caught with contraband himself and hanged for his crimes. It is believed that he was buried outside the church walls, as criminals were deemed unfit to be buried on consecrated ground. Could this be the ghost that Amir captured on his camera? Was it the corrupt judge who chased Amir and his team out of the churchyard that evening or could the person peering over the headstone be one of the smugglers who was executed for his crimes?

Whatever the reason for Amir's photo it certainly makes

a good story and I am sure would tempt any non-believer, like Amy, to rethink the paranormal world altogether. However, some might suggest that the ghost hunting team had been experiencing an everyday phenomenon known as face pareidolia: an ingrained ability to see faces in everyday objects. There is a theory that this trait is inbuilt within humans and may hark back to the days when homo sapiens were hunted by large predators such as sabre tooth tigers and they needed to be cautious of things lurking in the shadows.

It has been theorised that our brain can respond emotionally to these illusory faces in the same way it does to real faces. Whether it be a shape seen within a cloud, our morning cappuccino, or any object, humans appear to seek out faces in almost every situation. One woman in America was so convinced she had seen the vision of the Virgin Mary on her toasted cheese sandwich that she refused to eat it, called the local press, and eventually managed to sell it for a whopping $28,000. The sandwich, which was kept for over a decade before it was sold online, had not even a speck of mould on it when it was listed for sale, which the woman believes is proof that this was the mother of Christ on her lunchtime snack.

Sightings of the Virgin Mary have been witnessed across the world and there is an interactive map that can be found online that records areas of high activity. She has been seen by many people in the clouds, in hospitals, in churches, and on the side of apartment block buildings. She is said to appear to those who are devoted and faithful. Whether or not the Virgin Mary appeared on a slice of toast, or anywhere else for that matter, strange occurrences relating to death, religion, or the afterlife are likely to intrigue the human race for eternity.

Another interesting story that set me on a journey of discovery is the so-called 'Bleeding Gravestone of Hinkley'. Situated in the village of Hinkley, Lancashire, the gravestone in question belongs to a man called Richard Smith who was murdered on the 12 April 1727, in the village, and the stone is said to bleed red blood on the anniversary of his death. Richard Smith's story is quite a sad one, and I simply had to see if the stone did indeed bleed as the legend suggested. Making my way to Hinkley by train on 12 April, the exact date of the murder — albeit many centuries later—I made my way to the graveyard and set about finding the stone. It wasn't easy to locate and I had to ask a local for help. A gentle old man understood what I was looking for and, with the help of a few other locals, I eventually located the gravestone which, I was told, is not in its original location. Situated in St Mary's Church, the stone appeared well kept, which was slightly disappointing as the long train ride to Lancashire had made my mind wander with thoughts of the stone covered in blood just as the legend had suggested. The stone's inscription reads:

Here lieth the body of Richard Smith,
who departed this world on the 12th of April 1727,
In the 20th Year of his Age
A fatal Halbert his mortal Body slew
The murdering Hand God's vengeance will pursue
From shades Terrestrial, though Justice took her flight
Shall not the judge of all the Earth do right
Each Age and Sex his Innocence bemoans
And with sad sighs laments his dying Groans

The story of how Richard met his untimely death is so graphically recorded in his epitaph and, as the story details in part, poor Richard was murdered and died from a wound from a halberd. The headstone is intriguing and with further research, I learned what had happened to him that fateful day in April. Richard was in town and happily going about his business when he joined a crowd who had gathered outside a local pub to listen to an army sergeant's recruitment speech. The sergeant was called Simeon

Staynes, and he was standing outside a pub called the Pig and Whistle while trying to recruit men to join and fight for King and country. Richard began to mock the sergeant and taunt him with jokes. The crowd began to jeer and when the Sergeant suggested that the George Inn (now the Bounty) was named after King George I, Richard corrected him: the George Inn was actually named the George and Dragon. The crowd lapped it up and hollered and cheered with Smith who continued to poke fun at the sergeant. It all became too much for patriotic Simeon Staynes and he lost his temper.

Hoping to win back the crowd and silence the heckler, Staynes decided to demonstrate how a halberd is used in close combat. A halberd is a sharp axe-like weapon, which sits at the end of a long pole or staff and can be used to stab an enemy from far away. The sergeant lunged forward and, as a shocked crowd looked on, thrust the halberd deep into the young man's abdomen. Realising that he'd committed murder, Staynes fled the scene leaving Smith bleeding profusely in the road. The wound was fatal, but it took hours for Richard to die. As he slowly and painfully succumbed to his wound, a bounty was set for Simeon Staynes and he was later apprehended, tried for his crime, and sentenced to death.

As the sun was setting over the churchyard, I had a full opportunity to examine the headstone of Richard Smith. I could not see any red blood-like liquid, but I patiently waited for dusk to arrive — I am sure all things paranormal happen around dusk. But when the daylight faded there still wasn't anything to see on the stone. I did experience a cold chill in the air as day turned to night, but I was far from the South where I have lived all of my life and the Northern winds can be very cold. I also learned that the stone may — at one time — have sat upon a block of iron which could have reacted with the sandstone in certain weather conditions. This would cause it to leak a reddish, rust-like liquid that could be confused with blood.

The headstone had been moved from its original location to its present one many years ago, and there have been no recent reports of bleeding. I can only imagine that the stone may have had a chemical reaction to its surroundings or placement at some point in time. On the other hand, Richard Smith now rests in peace. Perhaps he no longer feels the need to scare visitors with a hemorrhaging headstone.

8 Curses & riddles

Apart from taphophiles, historians, and those paid to tender graves, few people spend their days off wandering around cemeteries. However, weaving through churchyards, reading headstones, and wondering about the stories of the people who once walked this earth is something I have always found fascinating, even if it can appear morbid to some.

Horror movies often depict cemeteries as places to fear. Movies show graveyards as places where a body can come back to life and cause harm to the living. Death is a taboo subject in many cultures. Those who have lost someone dear to them, often find it too hard to talk about or even think about their loss. Therefore, cemeteries are always going to be places that most people choose to stay away from. In the event of losing a loved one, many families only visit a person's grave on anniversaries or special occasions such as a person's passing date, their birthday or at Christmas.

Cemeteries — although many of them are now regularly maintained by strict council budgets — often show signs of significant decay, and care needs to be taken when passing through. A loved one's grave is sometimes left open to the elements and only tended to if a person's family has paid a third party to maintain it or tend to it themselves. Consequently, many cemeteries and graves are unkempt, overgrown, and unloved, which only adds to the spookiness of these places. Stories of unusual goings-on, especially in very old graveyards or ones that are home to ageing, crumbling or gothic style headstones, will more than likely continue forever.

One story that has hung around for centuries resulted in a grave being covered in a Mortlake cage. These cages can be seen across the UK in various cemeteries but, for the most part, they remain rare. A Mortlake cage is a metal fence or cage, that completely covers a person's grave, with gaps too small to reach in. These cages are often added to a grave to reduce vandalism, but some cages have been put in place for a more sinister reason. There are various legends surrounding the metal cages which have been installed above certain graves and some were placed there to stop a corpse from rising.

One such story surrounds an ancient grave situated in the Scottish Highlands which is said to have had a Mortlake cage installed by the local council for another eerie reason. The grave belongs to a man called Seath Mor Sgorfhiaclach, who was the clan chief of the Shaw Clan, in the late 1300s. The grave is believed to be cursed and many who have doubted it have suffered serious consequences by merely touching it. Known locally as 'The Great Shaw', Seath Mor died a hero many years after a bloody battle which only he survived. In Perth, Scotland, in 1395, a feud broke out between the Shaw and the Grant Clans. A dispute arose after one of the Shaw clan's notables died and was buried in a traditional resting place. A few days later, members of the Grant family, who had only recently moved into the area, knocked on the door of the deceased man's wife. When she opened the door, she found her late husband's decaying body had been propped against the door by members of the Grant clan, who fled before they could be identified

The body fell into the house, deeply distressing the widow and convincing the clan elders that they had to respond. Desecrating a clan member's grave was a huge dishonour but exhuming a man of nobility and taunting his grieving wife with his body was too much for the Shaw clan. A fight to the death was arranged which would be fought in front of King Robert III. The battle was bloody, arduous, and drawn-out. Thirty men took part and the last man standing was Seath Mor.

He was a powerful, tall man with striking red hair and a crooked grin that could strike fear into the hearts of even his own people. Surviving the deadly conflict, Seath Mor returned home to his family, having lost all of his comrades that day. He went on to live for a further fifteen years and finally died in 1405, taking his hero status with him. His grave lies in a cemetery situated deep in ancient woodland on the Rothiemurchus Estate in the Scottish Highlands. His legend lives on and over the centuries there have been many reported sightings of Seath Mor in the place where he has rested since 1405.

It is said that anyone who encounters his spirit, is challenged by the brave fighter to an imminent battle. If you run from the ghostly apparition, you will never be seen or heard from again, but if you accept his terrifying challenge, the ghostly figure disappears to leave you in peace. But this isn't the most frightening part of the legend of Seath Mor's grave, nor the reason behind the installation of the Mortlake cage. Several cheese-shaped stones were laid on top of the grave when Seath Mor was buried in 1405, and the stones were intended to represent the men who had fallen that day in the battle that Seath Mor so famously escaped from.

In recent years there have only been five stones present on the grave, but twenty-nine men lost their lives that day in the battle, and locals say that there used to be more than five stones. Stories from the locality report that those who have tampered with the stones have quickly gone on to suffer serious illness and in some cases mysterious and often imminent deaths. Moving the stones is not something the locals recommend, and if the cursed cheese-shaped boulders were not enough to frighten visitors away from this ancient memorial, the grave is also said to be guarded by another spirit called the Bodach an Duin — an elf-like creature who has a horrifyingly bad temper. A Bodach is an old man, or bogeyman, a figure which has been detailed in Gaelic culture for centuries. My father used to scare us as children by telling us that if we didn't go to sleep, the Bodach will get us! Of course, we knew he was playing and, if anything, it made my siblings and I shriek with laughter, while running into our beds and hiding under the covers as my father chased us up the stairs, pretending to be the Bodach.

This type of entity is talked about often amongst some Celtic people and it is thought to be a trickster type of spirit that should not be trusted. The Bodach Glas is another similar entity within Irish culture, which is said to bring about death, so fear of a Bodach runs deep through Celtic society. Moving stones on top of an old grave and succumbing to illness or death sounds a little far-fetched, however, these stories are not as ancient as the grave itself. Despite the warnings of the well-known legend surrounding this time-worn monument, there were still those who wished to push their luck and disturb the stones, although they may have later wished they hadn't.

The first reported incident regarding the removal of the stones was from an unknown date but tells of a man who one day decided to take one of the stones from the grave and toss it into the nearby River Spey. The man whose name has been lost in time, is alleged to have been found dead, face down in the river just a few hours after the theft. A second death relating to the stones occurred in the 1940s when a journalist investigating the curse removed one of the stones while mocking the legend of the Seath Mor. At the same time a small group on a field trip were visiting the cemetery. Lifting the centre stone high above his head, he declared that the curse of the stones was nothing more than local gossip designed to bring more tourism to the area. Newspapers reported that the journalist died in a horrific car accident on that very same day.

The curse continued over the years but there always seemed to be sceptical people who were hell-bent on proving the curse to be a ruse. In 1978, a man called Lesley Walker and his two friends were brought in to renovate the churchyard of Doune, where the grave is situated. Walker manhandled one of the stones by turning it around to show the others. He was interviewed by the *Aberdeen Express* just a few hours later, but afterwards he fell ill with a mysterious illness. He suffered from a burning fever and had to be hospitalised for over six weeks; reportedly losing around three stones in weight.

Another of the workers who was with Walker in the cemetery went a few steps further by completely rearranging the stones. He was found dead in the graveyard less than 24 hours later, having suffered a brain haemorrhage. The third worker was called in to identify the body of his late colleague, and it was said that he too went on to suffer a misfortune. He'd played no part in touching the stones, but he is believed to have suffered from crippling stomach pains shortly after identifying the deceased man.

The last attempt to test the legendary curse of Seath Mor was in 1982 when all five stones mysteriously disappeared from the top of the grave one rain-soaked night. Locals gossiped over who could have removed them, but there were no reported deaths or mysterious illnesses in the area. The stones miraculously reappeared a few nights later, seemingly undamaged and placed in the same position that they were in before they disappeared. One year later, in 1983, the local council decided to install a Mortlake cage to avoid any further vandalism or high-jinx. The five cylindrical stones now sit below the cage and due to the tight-knit structure of the iron fence, visitors can no longer move or touch the stones. There have been no reported attempts to disturb the stones since, but the legend of Seath Mor and the spirit who guards his grave, lives on.

Curses have been bestowed upon graves since the dawn of time. Warnings, spells and curses, feature heavily in Egyptian tombs and tablets. A magic spell carved deep into a gravestone or tomb wall, warning of falling ill or succumbing to an untimely death, is a great way to ward off any body snatchers or grave-robbers and is sure to last the test of time. William Shakespeare himself even had a curse inscribed on his headstone, perhaps to ward off any trophy hunters after his passing in 1616. The epitaph on the grave, which is minus his name simply reads:

Good friend, for Jesus' sake forbear,
To dig the dust enclosed here.
Blessed be the man that spares these stones,
And cursed be he that moves my bones.

Despite the curse, there have been many rumours that theatre's most famous writer is missing a vital body part — his head. The Holy Trinity Church, where Shakespeare and his wife Anne Hathaway are buried, has received hundreds of requests over the centuries to exhume poor old William Shakespeare, but permission has never been granted as it would result in much disruption to the ground and to the church. However, permission was recently granted for a group of anthropologists to perform a radar scan of the grave within the church, which is located in the playwright's birth town of Stratford-upon-Avon. The scan, which caused no damage to the grave, found that The Bard was, indeed, headless beneath the earth. His wife, and the other family members he had been interred with, appear to be fully intact but the famous playwright's head is missing. His body, minus the head, lies more than three meters below the ground.

The grave understandably attracts many visitors, and the epitaph only adds to the intrigue of the final resting place. The Shakespeare family curse, however, appeared to have not stopped grave robbers who must have removed Shakespeare's head many years ago. It was alleged that a group of grave thieves, led by a man called Dr Frank Chambers, broke into Shakespeare's tomb around 1794. The theft came about after Dr Chambers had attended a dinner party at Ragley House late one evening in autumn. Discussions about the famous writer began over drinks and ended with a challenge by one guest who offered three hundred guineas to any man who could bring him Shakespeare's skull. Chambers, who most likely had been drinking at the dinner party, decided to accept the challenge, and met with three accomplices on the corner of Malt Mill, Alcester. In the dead of night, the four men, Dr Chambers, Harry Cull, Tom Dyer and Jim Hawtin, crept into the church and located Shakespeare's grave. Removing the heavy slab that covers the grave, Chambers, who stood nearby, instructed the three men to dig with their hands, so as not to damage the grisly prize. A diary entry from Dr Chambers reads 'I handled Shakespeare's skull at last, and gazed at it only for a moment, for time was precious. It was smaller than I expected, and in its formation not much like what I remembered of the effigy above our heads'. The men then replaced the soil and the slab and very carefully made it appear as though the grave had never been disturbed. Chambers paid the men for their work and another diary entry reads 'afterwards paid for nine quarts of ale at the Globe, so that they seemed well satisfied with the night's adventure'.

Chambers is said to have gone on to sell the Bard's skull and, if he did receive the three hundred guineas from the man who made the pledge, it would equate in today's money to the princely sum of around £39,000. A recent radar scan shows that only the body of a man, thought to be that of

William Shakespeare, lies just a few feet beneath the earth, sans skull. Perhaps the curse was added after Shakespeare lost his head as a warning for other corpse thieves. Perhaps it was always there, and the tale of the drunken challenge is true. Whatever happened and wherever Shakespeare's skull resides now, we have more than enough to remember the great man by.

Another cursed grave that has kept visitors guessing for over two centuries is that of a married couple: James and Susan Thorneley. Their tombstone, which is situated in St Mary's Churchyard, Stockport reads:

> In Memory of James Thorneley of Stockport,
> died Oct 30th1823 aged One Thousand
> One Hundred and Forty-Five Moons.
> also Susan his wife who died July 22nd
> 1798 aged Seven hundred and
> Thirty-seven Moons.
> James Thorneley and his Wife lies under this stone
> And cursed is he that disturbs one bone.

The curse sounds strikingly similar to the one engraved on Shakespeare's grave, but the Thorneley's epitaph was carved by a stonemason over two hundred years later. Grave robbery and the sale of body parts were rife in the seventeen and eighteen hundreds, so much so that many families stayed up late to guard the grave of a loved one in the days after a person's passing, with some even sleeping on the graves or within the tombs themselves. Stories of zombies rising from a grave could often be explained by a groggy family member, waking up in the cold light of the morning, having just completed a night shift of guarding their loved one's grave, before switching with another family member. There had long been a demand for corpses in the medical training world and merciless robbers would exhume bodies to sell to students of anatomy.

The main source of bodies for medical dissection was

from criminals who had been convicted and executed, which was a law brought in by King Henry VIII, but as the world of medicine rapidly expanded and the industrial revolution took hold, demand for bodies increased. The shortfall was increasingly met by local gangs who saw no shame in desecrating a person's final resting place and snatching the corpse. These criminals were known as resurrection men, sack-em-ups, shusy-lifters, and noddies. In 1832, after many years of grave desecration and public outcry, parliament introduced the Anatomy Act, which required anyone wishing to practice anatomy to obtain a license from the Home Secretary.

The Act, which was strictly enforced across the country, stipulated that a person having lawful possession of a body may permit it to undergo anatomical examination provided that no relative objected. The Act provided for the needs of physicians, surgeons, and students by giving them legal access to corpses that were unclaimed after death, in particular those who died in prison or the workhouse. A relative could also donate their next of kin's corpse in exchange for burial at the expense of the medical professional. The Act also prohibited using the bodies of hanged criminals for medical research, and it finally put an end to the dark period of body snatching.

It's not surprising that Mr and Mrs Thorneley wished to be left in peace after their passing, but the inscription on their headstone which shows their lifespan in moons rather than years still gets visitors to the churchyard guessing. James Thoneley, apparently, lived for one thousand, one hundred and forty-five moons, while his wife lived for seven hundred and thirty-seven. Most calendar years have twelve full moons, however, every two and a half years or so, there is a thirteenth. On that basis I calculate John's age at the time of his death to be 93 and Susan's 60.

Perhaps the Thorneleys had an interest in astronomy or shared an interest in moon phases. Maybe they spent many nights huddled up together looking up at the moon with love in their hearts. Whatever the reason for their unusual memorial carving, this headstone will keep people guessing for many centuries to come.

Another fascinating gravestone which lies in St Anne's churchyard in the town of Buxton, is that of the famous 18th-century actor John Kane. He was born in Ireland in 1746 but moved to the Britain and became an actor and comedian of distinction. He honed his skills and created an act which was a type of costermonger personality: a cheeky chappie, cockney style character who was very popular. He was touring at the time of his death in a play called *Romp* which was being showcased at the Buxton Theatre. He was a man with an incredible appetite and had a particular fondness for roasted beef sandwiches with horseradish sauce. According to local legend, one afternoon in December 1799, during a break from one of his shows, he ordered his favourite sandwich from a local tavern. Tragically for Kane, the person who prepared the tasty treat had mistaken hemlock for wild horseradish while foraging for the ingredients of the sauce. Hemlock is highly toxic and can be fatal if ingested. However, hemlock and horseradish look quite dissimilar which made me wonder if water hemlock could have been the deadly culprit. Water hemlock, which grows close to the water's edge can often be mistaken for watercress which is an excellent addition to a roasted beef sandwich. Either way, both hemlocks are fatal if ingested and it appears that the curtain came down for the last time for unlucky John Kane.

Kane suffered an agonizing death accompanied by hallucinations, and violent convulsions. His grave is located at the back of St Anne's church and is now a listed monument. His headstone still attracts many visitors and was placed facing the rest of the graves in the churchyard so that the famous man, who was much loved by his audience, can continue to face the crowd, night after night forever.

9 Worked to death

There are around six million gravestones in England alone, and some twenty-five thousand are thought to be lost to weathering, relocation, and vandalism every year. However, those which attract attention, for one reason or another, often remain relatively intact due to their popularity. If, for example, a person was famous in their lifetime, their grave is likely to attract visitors to the cemetery, and if the grave falls into disrepair or is vandalised, local councils often pay to restore the memorial site, preserving it for future generations. However, a person doesn't have to have been famous or well known to attract visitors to their final resting place. Oftentimes a sad or unusual story is all that is required to help to preserve a person's legacy after their death.

I stumbled across a sorrowful story about a brave firefighter who sadly lost his life at work one day in the late 1930s. His passing, however, led to an almost immediate change in legislation for people working within the fire service across the UK. His gravestone is an interesting one, clearly advertising what he did for a job was when he was alive. The burial site and gravestone, which is in Poole Cemetery, Dorset, appears to have aged rather well. Either that or it has been cared for by surviving family members as the stone, which is made of white marble, glistens in the daylight and is still almost as white and as clean as the day it was carved. Buried beneath is Frank Phillips and, on top of a carved cube of white marble, sits a neatly sculpted fireman's helmet.

Frank was aged just 30 when he passed away in 1937, while on duty one tragic night in September, having attempted to tackle a fire in his hometown of Poole. On 8 September 1937, Frank and his brother Frederick — also a fireman — attended a fire in a row of wooden sheds in the Parkstone area of Poole. The fire had taken hold quickly and, due to the shed's timber composition, the roofs of the sheds had completely collapsed leaving electrical wires dangerously exposed. As the two brothers ran into the yard to tackle the fire, the top of Frank's brass helmet touched one of the overhanging wires, sending thousands of volts through his body. He was electrocuted and died instantly. He fell backwards onto his brother Frederick, who also received a powerful, but not fatal, electric shock. A third man tried to help the two stricken brothers and also suffered a mild electrical shock, but he and Frederick survived, escaping with minor burns.

Frank's tragic death hastened the change from brass helmets to reinforced leather, an improvement which had started to roll out across the Fire Brigade from 1934. But sadly, the change came too late for Frank who left a young wife, Mary, and two young sons Albert and Brian. His grave and its expertly carved headstone can be found towards the back of the cemetery, next to a beautiful row of laurel trees. Clearly loved within his lifetime his heart-wrenching epitaph reads:

In memory of my dear husband Frank Phillips (Judgee)
Killed on duty September 8th, 1937, aged 30
HE DIED AT HIS POST

It is not known why Frank's nickname or pet name was 'Judgee' but a friendly sobriquet added to a person's epitaph plainly shows that the person who passed away was loved and sorely missed. Frank Phillips died young and at a time in his life when he should have been enjoying his homelife and young family. The type of helmet he was wearing at the time of his death had previously been linked to other accidents, however, Frank's tragic death was the first and the last in relation to brass helmets. The terrible incident hastened the change and new leather helmets were distributed across the entire Fire service before any more lives could be lost. Firemen and women lead a dangerous career, but Frank and his family were let down by something that should have been replaced many months before.

Employers are now required by law to protect their employees from danger and millions of pounds are spent each year ensuring that the correct equipment is provided, and safety procedures are in place. Fatalities at work are rare but in 2021, National Health statistics reported that there were over 1.7 million work-related illnesses recorded in the UK. 142 people died in the previous 12 months of the census and the main cause of death at work was falling or overexertion.

Nevertheless, at the turn of the century, work-related deaths were commonplace and around four and a half thousand fatalities at work were recorded in 1900. Thankfully, working conditions have improved since then. Most deaths which do occur at work are accidents, but that was not always the case.

Hannah Twynnoy was a barmaid who lived and worked in the town of Malmesbury. She passed away in 1703 and is documented as the first person in the UK to have been killed by a tiger. Hannah was working in her local pub which was, ironically, called the White Lion. A passing menagerie had been set up in the substantial grounds of the pub. The visiting circus was a huge attraction and Hannah was busy serving drinks and food to happy customers who came to see the exotic animals and enjoy a beverage or two.

Hannah was said to have enjoyed poking the animals

with sticks, banging on their cages, and generally annoying them each day when she arrived for work. She had been warned several times not to be unkind to or to provoke the wild animals, particularly the tiger, who was kept on an iron chain-link leash bolted to the wall of the pub. The Siberian tiger was a male and weighed around 400lbs. Hannah had been seen many times, by her colleagues and pubgoers, poking the tiger with sticks, shouting at it, stamping her feet next to it and teasing it whenever she got the chance. As the weeks passed Hannah continued to taunt the animals despite warnings from her work friends and from the animal keepers.

One day, after poking the tiger several times with a large stick, the tiger snapped and launched its massive 400lb body towards her. Ripping the bolt from the wall and breaking free from its iron shackles, it tore into the barmaid. Her clothes were shredded in seconds and the tiger's blade-like teeth ripped the woman apart, limb by limb. Despite several attempts by others who bravely tried to save the poor woman, the beast mauled Hannah to death in a matter of seconds. Three centuries have passed since her untimely death but her grave still attracts regular visitors and is listed on websites and pages of historical interest. A tradition grew in which local girls with the name of Hannah left flowers by her grave on the anniversary of her death. Her small headstone can be found in Malmesbury Abbey churchyard with an epitaph that reads:

In Memory of Hannah Twynnoy
Who died October 23rd, 1703
Aged 33 years
In bloom of life
She's snatch'd from hence
She had not room to make defence;
For Tyger fierce took life away.
And here she lies in a bed of Clay
Until the resurrection Day

The tiger that attacked and killed Hannah was provoked by her daily taunts, but it is also likely that the animal was not best cared for by the travelling circus. A tiger needs to eat large quantities of fresh meat and — as they are highly intelligent animals — they need a lot of mental stimulation as well as a large enclosure in which to roam. It is highly doubtful that the habitual needs of the tiger were being met, and this, coupled with the heavy chain leash, would have likely been things that contributed to the death of poor Hannah Twynnoy.

A rumour surrounding Hannah's love life has flourished for centuries. She may have been having an affair with a person of nobility, as her gravestone could not be attributed to that of a pauper: it is expertly carved and made from an expensive material for the time. Whoever she loved in life, her stone remains a fascinating one for taphophiles, visitors, girls called Hannah and historians alike.

Just over a century after Twynnoy's untimely death, a well-known 19th Century lion tamer became the victim of a big cat attack while performing his famous circus act before a crowd of over five hundred. Thomas Macarte was a lion tamer who was born in Cork, Ireland, but who had travelled to England and began taking up work in various travelling shows. He became an apprentice lion tamer for a circus company called Messrs Bell and Myers and quickly moved up the ranks. Within a few years he was hired as the principal lion tamer for another popular travelling circus, The Manders Menagerie, which had set up in the marketplace of Bolton, Lancashire.

Thomas Macarte, who had adopted the stage name Massarti, had been hired to replace his predecessor, a man known as Maccomo, who had succumbed to a fever just one month prior. Maccomo was an African, born in Angola, and the first black man to become a lion tamer in Britain. He died of natural causes, but he had been mauled by the beasts many times. One night his replacement,

Massarti, was performing an unusual part of his popular act called 'The Lion Hunt'. This involved driving five male lions from one end of the stage to another while dressed as a Roman gladiator, but things didn't go according to plan.

Massarti only had one arm, having lost a limb while working as assistant to another well-known lion tamer, Alfred Moffat. In 1862, while working at The American Hippodrome Circus in Liverpool, Massarti had simply walked past a cage containing one of the circus lionesses, when he was seized by the left arm. The attack took just seconds, but his arm was so badly mauled, amputation was the only option. From that night on, Massarti no longer felt comfortable with the big cats and drank heavily before every performance. Maccomo, his predecessor, had been teetotal and probably knew that being drunk, and showing weakness around large predators, is almost always a recipe for disaster, but Massarti was earning £4 a week for his work; almost four times the average weekly salary of the time.

Massarti was famous for turning his back on the cats, but lions are ambush predators and thrive on taking their prey by surprise. In the week before his death, he had received a small but worrying bite. On returning home, he admitted to his wife that he was now terrified of the animals. Lions can sense the fear within their prey and are opportunists who instinctively exploit weakness. Running and catching prey takes up a lot of energy for a big cat so they will always try and find the easiest catch to use the least amount of energy.

In January 1872, during the well-rehearsed sequence of his 'Lion Hunt' act, Massarti was driving the animals from one end of the stage to the other when one of the cats ran against his leg, knocking him to the ground. The crowd cheered as he quickly jumped to his feet, driving the animals back into the corner as he had done so many times. He continued the act, and the next part involved stamping his feet to signal to the lion to run past him and into another corner of the stage, but as they ran past, one of the lions knocked him to the ground once more, striking him with his massive paw as he fell. The crowd cheered louder, assuming it was all part of the act.

This time Massarti only managed to rise to his knees but used a sword he was carrying to strike the lion as a warning. The lion backed away, but another lion lunged, tore Massarti's costume from his chest and pinned him to the ground. The crowd applauded, assuming that everything was planned and rehearsed. As one lion retreated, the four other lions attacked Massarti as he desperately used his revolver, loaded with blanks, to frighten the animals away. As the gun fired, the audience panicked, now realising that the act had gone horribly wrong. Women screamed and ran from the tent, scrambling for the exit with their children.

As Massarti lay bleeding on the floor of the ring, his frantic colleagues tried to reach him. But he was now surrounded by marauding cats. A large Asiatic lion with a huge black mane tore into his remaining arm, breaking every bone and ripping away the flesh. Brave men ran into the ring with pitchforks, broom handles, and swords. One of them managed to injure a smaller lion with a pitchfork and it retreated to a corner of the stage — known as the den — which contained the door to the lions' enclosure. With the audience running for their lives, the remaining men and circus staff continued to fight the lions with anything that lay to hand. Nevertheless, each time a lion fell away, another lunged forward to replace it, dragging poor Massarti ever closer to the door of the den.

Massarti's colleagues managed to pull him away but the lion who had first attacked him dragged him back and stood proud over Massarti once more, determined to keep his prize. The other four lions were forced back into the den but the fifth remained, roaring and snapping at anyone who came close to the heavily bleeding Massarti. Men with hot irons eventually appeared on the scene but they arrived almost a quarter of an hour after the initial attack. They thrust hot metal into the face of the lion, burning his nose and scalding his face, and he finally let go of Massarti and retreated into the den. But, just as the staff opened the door to force the last remaining lion back inside, another lion ran back into the ring, grabbing the lion tamer by the foot and mauling him again.

Finally, by using hot pokers and irons, they forced the remaining lion back into the den, carried Massarti out of the ring and took him to hospital, but there was little that could be done. His legs were badly torn and dripping with blood, his right arm was crushed and hanging off, almost all of his scalp had been torn away from his skull and he was bleeding profusely from multiple wounds. His last words were, 'I am done for', and he died on the stretcher in front of his colleagues.

Later that afternoon Massarti's wife arrived at the circus, worried that he had not returned home for his tea. She was met by the coroner who gave her the terrible news and asked if Massarti had taken any alcohol that morning. The coroner had already been told by others that he had been unsteady on his feet and swaying from side to side. She denied he had been drinking but others knew that Massarti had been using alcohol before every performance. The lion that first attacked Massarti may have known that he was frightened and would have waited until the lion tamer let his guard down. An inebriated lion tamer, would not have lasted very long against a pride of apex predators. The tragic story was covered in the *Manchester Evening News*:

> A very shocking affair took place last night in Bolton ... Part of the performance consists of a 'lion hunt', during the course of which five large lions are put through a variety of movements by a man, dressed in a French uniform [sic], whose name is given in

the bills as 'Massarti', but whose real name is Thomas
Macarte. Last night, about half-past ten o'clock, the last
representation in connection with the 'farewell visit' of
the establishment was given, and during its progression
Macarte slipped and fell to the floor while engaged in
a large cage with the five full grown lions. One of the
largest of the animals, a black Barbary lion, immediately
sprang upon him with a terrific roar and was quickly
followed by its companions. A horrible scene ensued.
Within the den a frightful tragedy was enacted, the cries
of the unhappy man struggling in the fangs of the savage
brutes, being scarcely heard amid their roaring. Outside
the cage a scene scarcely less appalling was witnessed. In
the large assemblage of visitors, stalwart men shrieked,
women tore their hair and fainted, and many were
unable to seek their homes until a considerable time
had elapsed. Macarte was rescued from the lions as
quickly as possible but ere this could be done he was
frightful torn by their teeth and claws, his legs, head,
and hands being lacerated to such a degree that the flesh
was completely torn away from the bones.

The savage death of Thomas Macarte (Massarti) made
headlines across the country, but tickets continued to sell
for similar shows as strongly as they had done before.
Following his death, in July of that year, Mrs Rosina
Manders, the owner of the Manders' Menagerie, who took
over the circus when her husband passed away in 1871,
paid for a beautiful and imposing monument comprising a
white marble cross nearly three feet high in memory of her
faithful worker. The Memorial can be found in the Roman
Catholic section of Tonge Cemetery in Bolton, with the
inscription:

*In memory of the great Lion Tamer, Thomas Macarte,
aged 34, killed at Bolton, Jan. 3rd, 1872, by the lions in
Manders' Star Menagerie. Erected to the memory of an
old and faithful servant by Mrs Rosina Manders, sole
proprietress of the Grand National Star Menagerie.*

'When thou hearest of a fellow mortal being suddenly plunged into eternity, think of the mercy that has spared thee.'

The African lion which had first attacked Macarte (Massarti) and which refused to give up the body when challenged in the ring, became known as the 'Macarte Lion'. Famous around the world, the fate of this lion was less dramatic than his victim's. When he died of natural causes in January 1874, the murderous 'Macarte Lion' still bore visible scars from the burning hot irons and sword cuts sustained during the fatal attack two years prior. Its corpse was taken to the renowned taxidermist, Rowland Ward, and was stuffed in a sitting position, baring its teeth in a snarl and mounted on a wooden base. A simple inscription read *A Wounded Lion*. It stood in the window of Ward's London shop for decades and attracted hundreds of visitors. The lion's current location is unknown, but there are several drawings online, and he even has his own Wikipedia page!

The 'Macarte Lion' was stuffed and displayed in a shop window.

10 Perpetual peace

As a teenager, I wore my hair long which I began to dye black around the age of 15. I had begun fashion modelling the previous summer and was told by my agent that there needed to be a difference between myself and the other models on the agency books, so I dyed my hair blue-black and returned a month later with new headshots for my agent, Karen. Her advice was sound, and I soon began to receive castings and jobs from local businesses — mainly hairdressers — but the combination of my new tresses and my very pale skin often led others to assume that I was a Goth.

I loved to wear black and my refusal to wear my navy-blue uniform at school — swapping it defiantly for black — probably fuelled the Goth image. All the same, I didn't spend my teens listening to Slipknot, or old tunes from The Cure. I preferred poems by Edgar Allan Poe and one of my favourite films happens to be Bram Stoker's *Dracula*.

I am a huge fan of Halloween, but I only own a few black clothes. By nature, I am optimistic, and I don't recall spending many of my school days feeling depressed, although I do vividly remember trying extremely hard not to smile, even when happiest. A huge fan of Oasis, I decided it was childish to smile and laugh and had seldom seen the Gallagher brothers smiling. I spent most of my final school days forcing a moody expression on my face, trying to look cool. The whole period now seems so very uncool, but I still do not believe I can pin my style down to that of a Goth. I did, however, recently stumble across a possible name for my style; 'Vanilla Goth', which describes a person who has a penchant for the macabre and unusual but who, nonetheless, dresses and acts conventionally.

Having said that, I did almost convince my partner to put a down payment on a house that used to be part of a church and still had graves and tombstones in the garden. It felt like a step too far for him, but another buyer pipped me to the post and snapped up the eerie property before I could make an offer. Looking deeper into the Goth culture, I discovered that there are, in fact, many genres of Goth including, hippie Goth, pastel Goth, casual Goth, and romantic Goth, so I am happy to be categorised under the genus of Vanilla.

I do enjoy soaking up the human stories of lives once lived by visiting a graveyard or two every now and again. I am inspired by the lives of those who walked the earth before, and I am not alone. Being moved by a dead person's backstory, is part of why I am intrigued by unusual headstones. Anyone with an imagination as vivid as mine would surely find it hard not to envision the life of the person before their extraordinary gravestone or unusual epitaph.

Few headstones offer the precise reason for a person's passing. There are exceptions, of course, but most require research into old archives — if they are still in existence or were ever created or kept in the first place. Either way, it is hard not to be inspired by the names, shapes, and words within cemetery walls. I can never resist visiting a new cemetery, especially if I am visiting a new town or city — assuming those I am travelling with agree — not everyone does. It is said that Charles Dickens came up with the name for his famous main character in *A Christmas Carol* while visiting a graveyard in Edinburgh where he saw the name 'Ebenezer Scroggie' carved into a headstone.

Bram Stoker set the most compelling part of his story *Dracula* in Whitby Cemetery, having been inspired by a visit to the Yorkshire seaside town in 1890. While seeking to purchase a holiday home in the area, Stoker visited the clifftop cemetery and was mesmerised by the crumbling tombstones and bat-infested ruins of the former Abbey. In the famous novel, Dracula finds himself in Whitby when the ship he was travelling in, the *Dementor* runs aground on the town's coast. Having devoured all but the ship's Captain along the journey, the Russian vessel smashes into rocks on the Yorkshire Coast releasing the count from his dusty, clay-filled box. One hundred and ninety-nine steps must be climbed before you can reach the cliffside churchyard, which overlooks the angry, cold, North Sea. If you watch the Hollywood movie of the fabulous gothic novel, a dramatic scene unfolds after the shipwreck which depicts Dracula in dog form, dashing up the steps, growling and panting before ravishing Lucy in further scenes by biting her neck and sucking her blood.

Thanks to Stoker, Whitby has become synonymous with the story of the blood-sucking count and thus has become a haven for Goths and horror fans alike. The bi-annual Goth Weekend, which attracts over 1,500 like-minded Goths, sees the streets littered with black and red-clothed revellers, sporting colourful hair, facial piercings, and steampunk hats. During the three-day festival, many revellers have been known to dash up the steps, climb aloft one of the tombs and remove several items of clothing before attempting to emulate the highly sexualised scene where Lucy, played by Sadie Frost in the Hollywood film, engages in a carnal and rather obscene sexual rendezvous with the count, who at the time is morphing further and is shown in terrifying werewolf form.

The festival attracts many photographers who, in recent

times, have complained about the abundance of flesh on show. It appears from one online blog that the local photographers have become somewhat bored of capturing busty women with their assets on show. Bram Stoker's novel may be fiction, but locals warn that you must keep your wits about you in Whitby cemetery. I often wonder if this is just a way of boosting tourism, or if it relates to an actual haunting, or is it because you could very easily get blown off the cliff by strong winds when visiting the ancient burial ground?

Many of the tombstones in Whitby Cemetery have succumbed to the harsh, salty North Sea winds or, as Stoker wrote, have been 'worn by the stress of years'. The tombstones appear to have melted away and, if you read Stoker's book, they were so back in 1890. Stoker's time here also inspired one of his main characters as he took the name of Mr Swales from one of the gravestones within the cemetery grounds. The stone is still there, attracting lots of interest at the Goth festival and throughout the year.

Swales became the Count's first victim in the gothic horror story. He is found with his neck snapped, sitting on a bench favoured by the two friends Mina and Lucy. There are paid tours, of course, to be found in the wonderful town, and many a local is happy to point visitors in the right direction of the cemetery and its crumbling stones. Dracula is obviously a fictional character not based on anyone buried here, and the famous writer who brought us this gothic masterpiece does not rest within the cemetery in Whitby either, much to the disappointment of misinformed tourists.

Bram Stoker is interred in Golders Green Cemetery, where he was cremated in 1912. The writer died from a series of strokes caused by a combination of exhaustion from overworking and, possibly, syphilis. Before the invention of penicillin in 1928, this sexually transmitted disease was a common cause of death. His death certificate recorded the cause of death as 'Locomotor Ataxis' which was often seen in patients with tabetic neurosyphilis at the turn of the century. Whatever the cause of Bram Stoker's death, his books remain among the most popular of the genre, and I challenge anyone to pick up a copy of *Dracula*, and not be engrossed from the very first pages.

There are many other unusual gravestones to see within the cemetery boundaries at Whitby, despite the difficulty of reading the faded, weather-beaten engravings. A lack of information, however, often helps to fuel the rumours behind a story, and preserve its legacy like that of the unusually shaped headstone, fondly referred to as 'Humpy Dumpty's Grave'. The flat oval-shaped or egg-shaped tomb sits close to the church wall and lies adjacent to an iron fence. The famous nursery rhyme never tells us what Humpy Dumpty was but most children and adults alike, refer to him as an egg, as books and cartoons have suggested over the years. The first reference of a half-human, half egg character in literature may come from the pages of Lewis Caroll's *Alice Through The Looking Glass*. But, the true nature of Humpty may predate Caroll's classic as other historians believe the riddle refers to a cannon which was placed on a wall in the town of Colchester and used to blast the enemy during the English Civil War. The conflict, which raged from 1642 to 1649, saw several cannons erected around the town to keep out Parliament's army, including one fondly named Humpty Dumpty which was, of course, sat on a wall.

Parliamentary forces heavily damaged the walls beneath Humpty Dumpty with their own artillery and it is believed that, when the wall collapsed and the cannon fell, the cumbersome, heavy gun could not be repaired, leaving the town of Colchester unprotected and paving the way for Cromwell's men to occupy it. Another rumour surrounding the children's rhyme refers to the falling of a Monarch. In the mid-1600s, the term Humpty

Dumpty was a common slang word for someone who was overweight. King Charles I sat on the throne at that time and was a little on the large side. Some historians suggest that the popular nursery rhyme could be attributed to the King's great fall from Parliament. All the King's Horses and all the king's men, could not save him from his downfall. Whosoever or whatsoever the name refers to, the legend of the egg-shaped tomb will likely continue to have visitors to the cemetery seeking out the egg-shaped grave, guessing who lies beneath, and keeping the nursery rhyme alive for many centuries.

Another well-known author who may also have been inspired by a local graveyard is Beatrix Potter. Born Helen Beatrix Potter, the celebrated children's author is known for living on a smallholding in the Lake District after purchasing a home there with the proceeds of the thirty books she penned. She was born in Kensington, London, in 1866, and spent the first part of her childhood at number 2 Bolton Gardens, which happens to be just two roads away from West Brompton Cemetery. Potter was well educated as were her parents and her grandfather was also a Member of Parliament. She illustrated her books, created merchandise from her characters, and her books were translated into several languages which continue to be sold worldwide, bringing delight to people young and old. Her first book, *The Tale of Peter Rabbit*, was rejected by six publishers so the plucky young lady self-published the sweet tale as a treat for just family and friends.

Peter Rabbit was born from letters she had written to a five-year-old child called Noël — the son of her former schoolteacher — who was recovering from scarlet fever. This legendary tale was an immediate hit with family and friends and the reviews spurred young Beatrix to re-submit the story to one of the publishers who had originally rejected it. Frederick Warne and Co published *The Tale of Peter Rabbit* in the summer of

1902 and by Christmas that year it had sold more than 20,000 copies.

The heart-warming story, however, and the character called Peter, may have macabre origins. In early 2001, James Mackay, who runs Friends of The Brompton Cemetery, was hoping to win lottery funding to preserve the graveyard when he stumbled across some interesting information in the digital archives of the cemetery. While building a profile for his application and hoping to find supporters who would help him secure a grant, Mackay discovered burial plots with names that appear in many of Potter's famous books. They included the grave of a Mr and Mrs Nutkin, another belonging to a man called Jeremiah Fisher, and several plots belonging to families with the surnames of Brock, Tod and MacGregor. But, when Mackay uncovered the burial plot of a man called Peter Rabbett, he knew he had stumbled upon something special.

Beatrix and her family were very fond of animals, having owned several family pets when she was a child. She was known to take her pets on holidays with her and it is well documented that she had a pet rabbit called Peter. Dates of the burial plots, almost all with no standing headstone, would have been old enough to be visible to a young Potter, assuming she had passed through the cemetery at some point during her time in London. While Mackay never found a burial plot or headstone for Mrs Tiggywinkle, or Jemimah Puddle-Duck, the connection to one of the world-famous children's authors and a London cemetery, shows that however young or old a person might be, inspiration can be taken from anywhere, even from graves.

When Potter died in December 1943 aged 77, she left almost all of her property and land to the National Trust and was herself was cremated in Blackpool. Her ashes were scattered on the land she owned by her property called Hill Top Farm, near Sawry in the Lake District.

PERPETUAL PEACE

Being a famous writer usually ensure a legacy after one's passing. Growing up in Bournemouth, I was always aware of a local connection to the writer Mary Shelley, author of the fabled novel, *Frankenstein; or, the Modern Prometheus*. I had heard an anecdote that her husband's heart was buried with her in St Peters Cemetery; a stone's throw away from my old employer's office. While working as a contracts administrator — before auditioning for drama school in the early 2000s — I had heard this macabre tale many times, but later discovered that Mary Shelley is, indeed, buried there in a family tomb, with her husband's heart beside her.

Mary was the wife of Percy Bysshe Shelley, the legendary romantic poet. The pair first met in 1812 when Mary was 14 and Percy 19. Percy had been invited by Mary's father, the writer William Godwin, to attend a dinner at the family home. Mary was immediately smitten, but Percy was already married to a 16-year-old bride. When Mary met him again, in 1814, they declared their love to each other during a visit to her mother's grave in the churchyard of St Pancras Old Church, and later consummated their affair in the very same place.

Mary's mother had died from puerperal fever shortly after giving birth, having caught it from the doctor who was trying to remove the placenta. Medics of the time often transmitted infections which led to puerperal sepsis in new mothers.

Mary frequently visited her mother's grave. The peaceful graveyard was semi-secluded, perhaps the perfect place to embark on a clandestine affair with a married man. Percy was not only married, but he had also recently become a father and was about to welcome a second child. William Godwin, Mary's father, forbade the romance and Mary vowed never to see Percy again, but when Percy threatened to commit suicide, the pair fled to France, taking a late-night crossing from Dover to Calais.

Percy had left his pregnant wife, Harriet, heartbroken. They returned to England two years later when Mary's half-sister committed suicide. Tragedy was to strike once more when, just a few weeks later, Harriet, Percy's wife, also took her own life. Her suicide, however, paved the way for Percy to marry Mary, and the two wed on 30th December 1816.

The couple eventually set up home in Italy. In July 1822, while Percy was making an ill-advised sea journey with two friends, their boat foundered during a storm and all three men drowned. Their bodies washed ashore ten days later and several of Percy's friends cremated the corpses themselves. Somehow, Mary Shelley's beloved husband's heart was untouched by the fire. One of his friends retrieved it from the pyre — burning his hand in the process — and sent it to his grieving widow. Mary wrapped it in silk with a parchment containing one of her husband's famous poems. She carried the heart with her always, until her own death in 1851.

A plaque was erected on the walls of the church where the family tomb lies, confirming that the author is buried there along with the heart of her husband. Two more blue plaques commemorate her life. One was erected in Marchmont Street where the author lived from 1815 to 1816 and another was erected in 2003 on the wall of number 24 Chester Square, Westminster, where the *Frankenstein* author lived between 1846 and 1852.

George Eliot's monument resides in Highgate Cemetery, in a lofty plot which at one time appears to have been lovingly tendered; established plants and shrubs still adorn the base of the marble obelisk. Eliot (whose real name was Mary Anne Evans) had hoped to be interred in Poets' Corner, along with other famous writers including Geoffrey Chaucer, Ben Johnson, and Tomas Hardy but, both her writing and the life that she led, were considered too controversial for Westminster Abbey. Despite publishing seven celebrated novels in her lifetime, Eliot was an unconventional atheist who lived with a man she was not married to. Her lover, George Lewes, did not divorce his first wife, Agnes Jervis, with whom he had an open marriage. In addition to the three children she had with Lewes, Agnes also had four children by Thornton Leigh Hunt. Eliot and Lewes lived 'out of wedlock' in an era when this was far from fashionable. It was not only George Eliot's adultery, but her refusal to conceal it which scandalised Victorian society and she was ostracised by much of it. She changed her name to Mary Ann Evans Lewes after George's death, and they are buried together in Highgate Cemetery.

JRR Tolkien, author of Lord of the Rings, is buried alongside his wife in Wolvercote Cemetery, Oxford. My father has a narrowboat moored along the canal in Wolvercote and was surprised to hear that it was the writer's final resting place. Tolkien had been in love with his wife since his early teens but was forbidden from contacting her until he was 21. By the time he had reached the age of his parent's consent, Edith was already engaged to another man. However, no sooner had Tolkien declared his love for Edith, than she called off the earlier engagement and the two remained married for fifty-five years.

The grave of children's author, Roald Dhal, can be found in St Peter and St Pauls Churchyard, in Buckinghamshire. It is rumoured that he was buried alongside some of his favourite things including chocolates, snooker cues, HB pencils, and even a much-loved power saw. Children leave gifts at the graveside, including copies of his books, lollipops, toys, and pens. Some schools even plan field trips to the author's final resting place, while taking in the museum dedicated to Dhal.

Jane Austen's grave lies in Winchester Cathedral. She had been living in Winchester for several months before her passing in 1817 and was often carried about the town in a sedan chair for short outings. The cause of her death had long been shrouded in mystery and, at the time of her illness, it was thought she had been poisoned with arsenic. However, scholars now believe that Austen died from Addison's disease, a malady that affects the adrenal glands, causing issues with heart function and blood pressure. In addition to her gravestone in the cathedral, a brass plaque was added in 1872 and a memorial window sometime later.

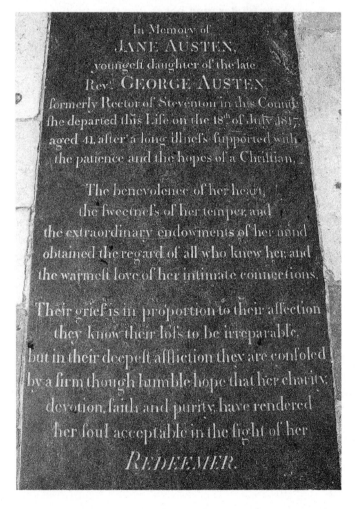

11 Faithful companions

For most of us, the passing of a loved one is utterly devastating, and it may take us years, or even a lifetime, to come to terms with it. For some, the passing of a pet can be equally painful. In the summer of 2018, we lost my beloved nine-year-old dog, Oscar, to a short battle with nasal cancer. He was a white, stout, miniature English Bull Terrier with an unusual temperament. When he became ill, my partner and I spent twelve thousand pounds of our savings on radiotherapy and other treatment, despite the grim outlook from consultant vets.

Oscar had a lot of energy, and we were shocked when he became so ill so quickly. Wanting to give him the best chance of survival, we opted to treat him but, in hindsight, it was selfish of us to have put our small dog through such a process. Despite several rounds of treatment, Oscar passed away in my arms one bright summer morning in our local vet's office. He had been a real handful throughout his life, often causing arguments between Bradley and I but he was also such a joy to be around, and stories of his japes are still recounted fondly by all who knew him.

English Bull Terriers are known for being clown-like and are fun and sweet dogs, despite their hard-looking exterior. Often depicted in films as thugs or evil dogs, they are anything but and are known to be mischievous and loving. Even Her Royal Highness, Princess Anne, owns a pack of EBT's as they are often referred to, and is said to be very fond of one of her dogs called Dotty. This dog, however, has been in trouble several times for biting children in Hyde Park and attacking one of the Queen's corgis, which subsequently had to be put to sleep. However, most EBT's are friendly and sweet, as Oscar was (most of the time).

Oscar had a strange way of deciding whom he liked and would often make a person beg for his paw or trick. The breed is known to be stubborn and often difficult to train but Oscar, despite his foibles, was very engaging and the neighbours loved him. They would often call his name as we walked by and he would always look up and give a tail wag, much to the delight of adults and children alike.

Family members joined us every birthday when we celebrated each year of his life with a specially made doggy sponge cake, paper hats, and toys. Oscar had been through so many different things with us as a family, from Bradley's first kidney transplant — which I donated — to its eventual failure a few years later, then failed IVF rounds which resulted in several miscarriages, two house moves, and finally the passing of Bradley's father, Albert, whom Oscar adored.

When Oscar died, we decided to have him cremated and I built a shelf in my kitchen where I placed his ashes and surrounded the little urn with photos and mementos of his life. Most people thought we were foolish to have spent so much money on a little dog and some thought I was silly to build a 'doggy shrine' for my pet, but this kind of sentiment for a deceased family pet is nothing new and I am not alone in how I chose to celebrate Oscar when he passed.

British people love their animals, and an estimated 34 million pets are currently living in homes across the UK. These animals often become beloved members of the family and when they pass away it can be heart-breaking. Today, many pet owners choose to cremate their pets and bring their ashes home. Some prefer to bury their pets in a quiet spot in their garden, but official pet cemeteries have been around for quite a while. Owners have been able to lovingly lay their pets to rest in private animal cemeteries since the late 1800s and there are more than fifty in Britain. The country's largest, in Ilford Park, London, has more than 3,000 animal burials: a mixture of family pets and military animals.

The first known pet cemetery was started by accident. Located in an obscure corner of London's Hyde Park, it was unofficially opened in 1881 when the park's gatekeeper, Mr Winbridge, was asked to bury a pet belonging to a friend. A much-loved dog named Cherry had died, and Winbridge agreed to bury him in the family's favourite corner of Hyde Park. A miniature headstone was placed on top of a small grave with the inscription 'Poor Cherry – Died April 28th, 1881'.

Royalty soon heard the news, and the next pet to be interred was a Yorkshire Terrier belonging to the Duke of Cambridge. The poor creature had been crushed beneath the wheels of a carriage — a common fate for dogs and cats of the time. Winbridge obligingly found a spot for the royal dog, and after the placing of the headstone, many more people asked if their pets could be laid to rest in what now amounted to a pet cemetery. When the graveyard closed, in 1903, over three hundred pets had been buried under miniature, mostly marble headstones, often with beautiful epitaphs. The headstones are still visible, but the cemetery is now closed to the public, except for occasional scheduled one-hour tours.

It is impossible not to be touched by the loving words that owners have chosen to honour their pets via their headstones: 'Topsey, loving until Death' and 'Our Sweet Bear Butch died 20th June 1891'. Honouring a pet in death became fashionable, and other pet cemeteries began to open around the UK. Headstones seldom provide much information on the passing of a pet, rather like their human counterparts, but some headstones found in pet cemeteries show an owner's sense of humour. One stone bears the inscription 'Morgan – aged 3 years, Slow mover, run over', and another is inscribed 'Vic — Had a fit, Died quick'. Another, in Welpe Park, reads 'Rector, Aged 4 years. Shot. 31st March 1890 — Ate without Stint, Lamb without mint'.

Less comedic headstones offer an insight into just how loved some pets were in life. Another tiny ageing stone in London's Hyde Park pet cemetery reads, 'Darling Dolly, My Sunbeam, My Consultation, My Joy.' The Victorian era is frequently viewed as a turning point in Britain for society's animal sentiments. During this time many animal welfare charities were founded, including the RSPCA, and attitudes to animals, their care, and their deaths changed dramatically. Nonetheless, owners have adored their pets for centuries and one touching tale of a man buried with his dog, in defiance of the Church, would only be uncovered many centuries later.

Sir Thomas Champney of Orchadleigh House, Somerset, died in 1839. His beloved dog, Azor, who had once saved his owner from drowning, had died and been buried many years earlier, but Champney's last will and testament required Azor to be re-buried 'at his feet'. Family members honoured his wishes and had the dog exhumed. Azor, who was a Pudelhund, or water dog, a breed similar to a German poodle, was reburied with Champney, as per his wishes. But, when the Bishop of Bath and Wells learned that a dog had been buried in consecrated ground, he was outraged and demanded its removal. The family had no choice but to comply and Champney's dog was exhumed for the second time and reburied in an adjacent field. A monument was erected with a headstone bearing several carved animal-shaped skulls above a tall base topped with a carved urn and drapery.

But the story was not over. In the 1980's, when planned restoration works were being carried out in the churchyard, the skeletal remains of a dog were found at Sir Thomas Champney's feet. In a move that will melt the hearts of all who love animals, the parish was granted what is known as a faculty (a right to undertake works on Church property) which permitted the dog to remain where he had lain for so long. Azor's monument, which had fooled the Bishop of Bath and Wells, was moved into the churchyard to rest for eternity with his master.

Another ancient grave which, for many, looks totally out of place, is a small headstone which can be found in Toxteth Park in Liverpool. It stands alone, surrounded by trees, and the engraving reads 'In Memory of Judy, who in 21 years service to this park was the children's friend, died 12th August 1926, aged 26.' Judy had lived 26 long years, and worked hard across the park, not just keeping children happy, but also helping the gardeners.

Judy was a much-loved donkey who, when the park was privately owned in the 1920s, had worked as a tourist attraction taking visitors and children on rides around the park. Judy must have been exceptional because, although she wasn't the only donkey, no other was honoured with a headstone in the park. Children would flock to ride her and often brought sweet treats which stained her teeth brown from her sugar addiction. She also worked as a helper, carrying loads on her back for garden clearances and was said to stop dead in her tracks on some journeys and could only be moved by the offer of a sugar cube. Judy lived and grazed in the park, retiring from her duties in 1924, but continued to be visited by children until her death in 1926.

Losing a pet to an accident, or even old age, is something that pet owners dread. During World War Two, however, in preparation for food shortages, over

750,000 British pets were euthanised in one week. During the summer of 1939 a pamphlet was sent to all UK households which read: 'If at all possible, send or take your household animals into the country in advance of an emergency.' It concluded: 'If you cannot place them in the care of neighbours, it really is kindest to have them destroyed.' Pet owners flocked to their local vets' offices to humanely euthanise their pets. Many chose to memorialise them with a newspaper acknowledgment. One heart-wrenching notice read, 'Happy memories of Iola, sweet faithful friend, given sleep September 4th, 1939, to be saved suffering during the war. A short but happy life — 2 years, 12 weeks. Forgive us, little pal.'

In the dire circumstances of a global war, it is understandable that the British public obeyed the notice that was given by parliament. Yet not all pets were culled, and many people continued to keep dogs, cats, and birds throughout the Blitz. Dogs were also required as rescue animals and many had served on the battlefield. Just two years after the terrible cull of 1939, a recruitment advert was placed in British newspapers asking for dogs to be placed into service. Within the first two weeks, over 7,000 dogs were put forward by their owners, and one Alsatian cross, called Bing, was dropped into France as a 'paradog', later receiving the PDSA Dickin Medal, introduced to honour the work of animals in the war.

'Faithful to the end' is often a compliment given to pets, particularly dogs, and one man who honoured his pet after death did so in a very unusual way. A monument in London's Highgate Cemetery has become fondly known as the 'Dog Grave', but it doesn't contain the body of an animal. It is the last resting place of one of London's most famous eighteenth century bare-knuckle boxers. Thomas Sayers was famous for winning almost all of his fights. He fought 16, won 12, drew 4, and lost just one which ran for a staggering 60 rounds! Sayers loved his pet dog so much that he chose to include, within his monument, a life-size stone carving of his mastiff, Lion, which sits for eternity at the end of his tomb.

Sayers was aged just 39 when he died of tuberculosis. Having fought in the weeks before his death, fans noticed that he appeared weak, thin, and haggard. He took to his bed in April 1865 just a few months after his final fight. When he passed away, the public flocked to witness his funeral, and reports suggest that over one hundred thousand people lined the streets on the day that his body was interred at Highgate Cemetery. Also joining the funeral procession was Sayer's dog, Lion, who sat alone in a pony cart during the funeral procession. One of the greatest of all bare-knuckle boxers, Thomas Sayers was posthumously inducted into the International Boxing Hall of Fame in 1990.

A recent archaeological dig undertaken in Sweden is thought to have uncovered the oldest pet burial ever discovered. The grave, which is thought to be around 8,500 years old, contains the remains of a dog who was buried along with what appears to be its owner. The stone age pair were found resting side by side and were both incredibly well preserved for their age. In ancient times people were often buried with items of value, importance, or great personal significance. However, the sentiment behind this particular burial appears to be unique for the period.

Dogs have been man's best friend for centuries and even our late Queen Elizabeth honoured her royal pets with burial in dedicated areas of Sandringham and Balmoral. The most recent interment was for one of the royal corgis called Monty, whom the Queen was particularly fond of. He appeared with her Majesty in the opening ceremony of the 2012 Olympic games in a now-famous comedy sketch with the James Bond actor Daniel Craig. Monty passed away aged 13 and a headstone bearing his name sits on top of the small grave amongst a long line of other Royal pets including Corgis, Labradors and spaniels. Each headstone has the words 'Faithful companion to the Queen' inscribed on them.

Heart-warming stories of special pets have been around for centuries, yet one tale, that of a little dog called Bobby who came to be revered as the essence of man's best friend, may have had its roots in an ingenious tourist attraction scam. Greyfriars Bobby was a little Skye Terrier who was said to have mourned the death of his owner by refusing to leave the gravesite long after his master had passed away. The legend inspired many books and films, but it actually began as local gossip. As word began to spread, so visitors flocked to the cemetery and the site where little Bobby, reportedly, waited for his master to wake.

The dog, who in truth may have been a stray, quickly became a celebrity and many of the visitors who came to see him brought food, blankets, and collars. A few generous visitors even donated money to pay for a guardian. So popular was Bobby that the town of Greyfriars saw a significant increase in tourism. The story of Greyfriars Bobby charmed the British public but research shows that there may have been two, or possibly more Bobbys kept at the graveyard. Photographs seem to show at least two different-looking dogs and some reports suggest that, in the beginning, when visitors came to see Bobby, he was a calm and sweet-natured dog, but later in life he appeared to the public as an aggressive and stubborn little animal.

Whatever the truth behind the story, locals believe that Bobby began life as a stray pup who was taken in by a man called John Grey who worked as a police nightwatchman. Bobby became Grey's faithful companion, accompanying him on his night watch as he walked the streets of Edinburgh. When John Grey passed away of tuberculosis, it was believed that little Bobby refused to leave his master's grave after the funeral and sat by it for over 14 years.

The streets of the UK were awash with stray dogs and

cats in the mid-1800s, and many dogs would frequent cemeteries as a place of shelter. Overrun with mice and rats, graveyards offered a regular food source. Often befriending a night watchman, or custodian of the church, little dogs frequently sat and waited for someone to come and pet or feed them.

A statue of Greyfriars Bobby now sits on top of a water fountain in the city, and the tale of one of the world's most faithful canines lives on. There have been many stories since of dogs and cats mourning the loss of their owners. Pet cemeteries, and the histories of dogs like Bobby, remind us of the importance of companion animals in our lives and owners will want to memorialise them for centuries to come.

12 Smooth criminals

Humans are the most highly evolved beings on our planet, and we are unique in being able to anticipate death. However, even when a person is diagnosed with a terminal illness, it can still be difficult to picture the end of life. Cemeteries, funeral homes, headstones and memorials are all means of honouring a loved one after their death. No matter how elaborate or simple a headstone or memorial is, there isn't much that separates us when the final curtain falls. Rich or poor, good or bad, we all face death at some point in our futures.

Despite the countless vampire movies, horror novels and paranormal investigations which have been set in graveyards, cemeteries are intended to be places of rest, reflection and sanctity. Consecrated ground, however, is not the exclusive reserve of those who have lived blameless lives. Many of Britain's most notorious criminals — even those who have committed atrocities — have been buried alongside law-abiding folk.

In December 1922, the Prison Commission ruled that the graves of executed criminals would no longer be marked by their names or initials. They feared that marking the grave of a high-profile criminal would cause unnecessary suffering to surviving victims or their relatives. Consequently, many criminal's graves lie within prison grounds, marked only by a date and number.

More recently, however, some of Britain's most infamous offenders have been allowed cremations and some have even been buried in churchyards. The notorious child killer, Ian Brady, was convicted of multiple murders in 1966, not long after the abolition of capital punishment. He was sentenced to life imprisonment for the torture and killing of five children and died in prison in 2017. It is believed that Brady's final wish was for his ashes to be scattered on the same moors where he had killed and buried his victims. His body was cremated during a private ceremony at Southport crematorium, but his ashes were scattered at sea. A request to play Berlioz's *Symphonie fantastique* during the ceremony was rejected by a judge.

Brady's accomplice, Myra Hindley, was granted an almost normal funeral. The city of Cambridge permitted a short service, with music and flowers, conducted by a priest at the Cambridge crematorium. Motorists blew their horns in protest at the hearse that carried her coffin, while a local woman pinned an A4 sheet of paper to the door with the words 'Burn In Hell' written in bold. The service was attended by 12 mourners, 25 police and almost 50 journalists. Hindley's coffin was adorned with flowers and a mass for the repose of her soul was conducted. Her ashes were handed over to family members after the ceremony.

Serial killer Fred West, together with his wife Rose, murdered more than ten young women including two of his own children. He committed suicide in Birmingham's Winson Green prison on New Year's Day 1995, before he could stand trial for his crimes. Controversially, he was permitted a funeral and cremation outside prison. Officials tried unsuccessfully to keep the location and time secret, but news soon broke that his funeral was to be held at Canley Crematorium, in Coventry. Locals were outraged when they learned that he was to be cremated alongside 'good and honest' residents of the city. There was no eulogy, hymns or flowers and just a handful of close relatives attended, including West's son and daughter.

His ashes were taken to Barry Island where, like Ian Brady's, they were scattered into the sea.

I was filming in the historic town of York when, during a break in the schedule, I came across a small patch of land with a large headstone located under an ancient sycamore tree. I knew of York's links with the infamous highwayman, Dick Turpin — there are nods to him all over the city — and I discovered, on closer inspection, that this was Turpin's headstone. There were, in fact, many others, but Turpin's was the only one standing; the rest had been used as flagstones to form a pathway. The inscription reads:

> John Palmer, otherwise Richard Turpin
> The notorious highwayman and horse stealer
> Executed at Tyburn, April 7th 1739
> and buried in St George's Churchyard.

Dick Turpin was tried at the York Assizes in March 1739 and sentenced to death by hanging. He was taken to the 'York Tyburn' at Knavesmire, wearing a new frockcoat and shoes so that he would look stylish. He even paid five mourners to follow his cart. Turpin spoke calmly to the hangman, bowed to the spectators, and threw himself off the ladder.

Nevertheless, an investigation by James Sharpe, Professor Emeritus of Early Modern History at the University of York, has cast doubt on Turpin's true resting place. Sharpe pointed out that convicted felons were rarely buried in marked graves, and all the other gravestones in the tiny cemetery date from well after Turpin's death. More importantly, there is no record of the gravestone before 1918.

Contemporary accounts say that Turpin was, indeed, buried in the churchyard of St George's, but body snatchers broke into the grave and carried away the corpse, aiming to sell it for medical research. They were thwarted by a mob, however, and the body was recovered. To prevent the grave being robbed again the coffin was filled with slaked lime which would have broken down the corpse quickly and made it unusable for dissection. It seems unlikely, therefore, that Turpin's remains really are under the gravestone that we see today. Like Greyfriar's Bobby, Turpin's headstone may have been created as a tourist attraction.

The graves of the notorious gangster twins, Ronnie and Reggie Kray, can be found — with lifelike etchings of the two men on the headstone — at Chingford Mount Cemetery in London. The brothers ruled the East End with iron fists in the 1950s and 1960s. Ronnie died in Broadmoor in 1995, and Reggie died of cancer five years later, just days after receiving compassionate release from prison. Both are buried, along with the Krays' older brother Charlie and the Krays' parents, Violet and Charlie Snr, in a family plot.

The funeral of Reggie Kray, the last member of the family to die, was a shadow of earlier Kray send-offs. It is true that 2,500 people turned out to watch his last journey along the

Bethnal Green Road, but when the twins' mother, Violet, made the same trip in 1982, more than 60,000 people had lined the route. There was a similar number for Ronnie, a few years later, and even brother Charlie — a relatively minor criminal — had drawn a large crowd, but Reggie's cortège raised less of a stir. Londoners seemed to have tired of gangster interments, possibly because there were no longer any living Krays to be seen.

13 Time travel

The word taphophilia sounds bizarre, almost like a condition or an ailment. In truth, when I first heard the term, I too found it strange. I had not previously known that my hobby had a name, but it is reassuring to know that I am not the only one interested in graves, graveyards, funerals, and the afterlife. When my father took us on family trips to St Mark's Cemetery in Talbot Woods, Bournemouth, I really was not a fan. Terrified in the back of the old Morris Minor, I questioned my father's sanity for taking us on such trips. All the same, dad is a huge history buff, studying the subject — along with politics — at Oxford Brookes University.

Every cemetery is full of history and religion, even a little politics. In fact, even the layout of a graveyard can be influenced by class, race or sect. It seems that my father has passed on the gene of 'tombstone tourist' to me because, if I am ever in a new town or city, I simply have to visit its cemeteries. Many grave hunters like to take gravestone rubbings using wax and paper. I have never done this but being able to soak up an array of architecture, art, and history — in most cases for free — is a bonus for anyone interested in the subject.

The other side of my interest lies in the mysteries that surround death. The paranormal and the great unknown have fascinated me ever since I stumbled across some back copies of a magazine in my parents' bedroom when I was around seven or eight years of age. The title was *The Unexplained: Mysteries of Mind, Space, & Time*, and the journal dealt with enigmas including UFOs, the Bermuda Triangle, ghosts, spontaneous human combustion, ancient knowledge, stone circles and even contact with the dead.

I vividly remember being terrified by a realistic depiction of the Devil on one of the front pages. My mother warned me not to look through the magazines as she feared I would have nightmares, but I couldn't help thinking that — had she not given me the warning — I wouldn't have crept into her room to find them. Curiosity and intrigue got the better of me and, as I thumbed through the pages — mostly while looking through the gaps in my fingers — I saw grainy photos of UFOs, little snippets on stories of alien encounters, terrifyingly realistic reader photos of ghosts and stories of devil worship.

My mother was right, I shouldn't have looked at the magazines. That night I went to bed confused and terrified but what I had seen sparked a lifelong search for more information on the mysteries of the world. My interest in cemeteries (not to be confused with the mental condition coimetromania: an abnormal desire to visit cemeteries and graveyards) led me to a curious monument that has, for years, been the subject of myth. The tombstone in London's Brompton cemetery is often referred to as 'The Courtoy grave' but is also known locally as 'The Time Machine'. Needless to say, when I heard about this extraordinary grave, I simply had to find out more.

There are several mysteries that surround this monument, one being that it doesn't appear on the blueprint plans for the cemetery, nor is it listed as a plot in the church archives. This, in itself, is remarkable because you simply cannot miss such a large piece of funerary architecture. It was built on a crossroads within the cemetery and such junctions have an important place within the paranormal. They are believed to be points of great energy, or portals to other realms or even times, and to be where the veil between this world and the next is the thinnest.

Crossroads within graveyards are said to be particularly powerful as well as unusual, because burial at a crossroads was usually reserved for those whose spirits were feared. There is an ancient belief that if the dead person's ghost rises from a crossroads grave, it will be confused, not know which road to take and, therefore, be unable to return and haunt the living. However, the location of this monument, rising up from its own circle of land, is just one of the clues leading some to believe that it is not a tomb at all, but may have an even deeper meaning.

It was built for Hannah Peters, a maidservant who was born around 1784 and left home early to escape an abusive father. She found employment with a wealthy and elderly ex-wig maker named John Courtoy. He grew fond of her and, despite being well into his seventies, fathered three children with her (or so he believed, there were no reliable paternity tests at that time). The couple were never married, but Peters took his surname and, upon his death, inherited a huge fortune: the equivalent of many millions in today's money.

Now a very wealthy woman, she met and became friends with Joseph Bonomi, a celebrated architect known for his Egyptian-influenced designs. Egyptomania had gripped the world — particularly Britain — in the Victorian era, thanks in part to Napoleon's invasion of the region. Egyptian antiquities, some real and some fake, became popular and fashion soon took note. Interior design, book covers, jewellery, pottery and architecture all began to feature Egyptian motifs. Burials soon followed, with pyramid designs featuring in many graveyards along with pharaohs, sphinxes and hieroglyphs.

The Western entrance of Highgate Cemetery is called Egyptian Avenue for obvious reasons. Obelisks, in particular, had become fashionable memorials. Cleopatra's Needle was brought from Egypt to London in 1887 and placed on the newly constructed Victoria Embankment. When Hannah died on 26th January 1849, in Belgravia London, Bonomi set about creating an opulent Neo-Egyptian tomb for his friend and, ultimately, two of Courtoy's unmarried daughters.

The mausoleum is one of the most imposing in London and the hieroglyphs which adorn the heavy bronze door add to the intrigue of this unusual grave. Scarab beetles can be clearly seen within the design and they, in Egyptology, are viewed as a symbol of rebirth and renewal. It is believed that this little beetle is linked to the god of the sun, who was thought to be reborn in the form of a winged scarab beetle every morning at sunrise. Alongside the beetles, sunburst shapes can be seen cast into the bronze door and there are small wheel shapes along the bottom designed to let in light from the morning sun.

The carvings around the door resemble tied bamboo, making this tomb appear almost as if it has been plucked straight out of Cairo. The ancient message on the tomb refers to enteral life, rebirth, and renewal, ideas heavily entwined in Egyptian culture. However, some believe that the tomb also contains the inner workings of a time machine or teleportation device, and its absence from the church plot plans only helps to fuel the centuries old rumour.

Bonomi, who died in 1878, is also interred in the cemetery and his grave can be found just a few yards away from Courtoy's. His headstone includes a carving of the Egyptian god Anubis: the jackal-headed god of death. Anubis was thought to protect a tomb or grave and is often depicted as a man with the head of a dog or jackal, or a fully formed jackal in a lying position, such as a dog would adopt when in guarding mode.

Close by lies the body of Samuel Alfred Warner who

was a celebrated inventor of the era but is today regarded as a fraudster. Introduced to Courtoy by Bonomi, Warner professed to have invented an 'invisible' shell, capable of destroying ships at sea. Today, however, this claim is thought to have been an elaborate hoax. Courtoy's tomb was completed in 1854 and is made of solid, polished granite. Her initials adorn the door, and the twenty-foot structure is topped off with a huge carved pyramid. The key to the tomb was lost many years ago, an intriguing fact for many grave lovers and historians who would love to find a replacement.

Bonomi and Warner persuaded Hannah to finance a secret — and probably fraudulent — project to design a time machine disguised as a mausoleum. One of the problems with such a device is that if you travel into the future, you cannot be sure what your surroundings will be when you arrive. Cemeteries, however, rarely change their locations and are not places of high footfall. Hannah died five years after the tomb's completion in 1849 and Warner died a short while after in suspicious circumstances. He lies in an unmarked grave — unusual for a man of his rank — and his death is shrouded in mystery. Some believe that he was killed by Bonomi to prevent him revealing the secrets of the time machine, and others have even suggested that he is not dead at all, but that he teleported himself to another time or dimension. Until a key is found, Hannah Courtoy's elaborate tomb will keep grave lovers and historians guessing.

In the village of Hardingstone, Northamptonshire, there is a simple wooden cross with the inscription: 'In Memory of an Unknown Man – Died November 6th, 1930.' The cross, which has been the only official marker of the grave since the interment of the body, marks the final resting place of a man who has never been identified and who, tragically, was the victim of another man's attempt to fake his own death.

TIME TRAVEL

On the morning of 6 November 1930, two men from the village of Hardingstone reported seeing a neatly dressed man, carrying a small suitcase, walking away from the town centre as they made their way into it. One of the men had seen an orange glow in the distance, which appeared to be a fire. That was not entirely surprising because it was the day after Guy Fawkes night. Nevertheless, when they approached the stranger, they asked him if he knew anything about it. The three chatted briefly and the stranger suggested that the fire had been lit by someone still celebrating bonfire night, albeit a little late. Accepting the plausible explanation, the men parted ways and the stranger continued his journey out of the town.

However, still concerned by the fire, which was now burning brightly on the horizon, the two men decided to investigate and discovered a blazing Morris Minor car. They put out the flames with water from a nearby pond only to discover a figure sat in the driver's seat. At first, they thought it was a Guy Fawkes dummy but, as the inferno subsided, they were horrified to see that it was the badly charred corpse of a man.

The police soon found evidence that the car had been deliberately torched, and a post-mortem examination of the deceased showed that he had died within 30 seconds of the blaze. Because no smoke was found inside his lungs, and a wooden mallet with human hairs attached was discovered close to the car, foul play was suspected. Police were also able to recover the remnants of a number plate from the wreckage which, after further investigation, showed that the car belonged to a man named Alfred Rouse.

A national search for the well-dressed stranger who had been seen that cold November morning was soon underway. There were appeals for the 'man with the suitcase' to identify himself, but nobody came forward. When police called at Alfred Rouse's home, however, they were told that he was away on business, but his wife confirmed that the car did belong to her husband. His work as a travelling salesman had been so successful, she claimed, that they had been able to purchase both a new home and a new Morris Minor car, in the summer of that same year. Mrs Rouse also identified her husband's badly burned wallet but could not identify the remnants of clothing found on the body.

Enquiries eventually showed that Rouse had hitchhiked from Northampton to London on the morning of the fire, but later travelled to Wales to visit one of his many mistresses, one Phyliss Jenkins. Police took a statement from Miss Jenkins who, after watching the national news, recognised the burned-out car as Rouse's. Jenkins, who was pregnant with Rouse's child, told the officers that Rouse had arrived at her home on the evening of 6 November, claiming that his car had been stolen. The couple were planning to get married but, when she saw the news reports after Rouse had left her home, she contacted the police.

Rouse was arrested while getting off a train in London and claimed that he was, at that very moment, on his way to report the theft of his car to the police. His explanation was that he had picked up an inebriated hitchhiker and a fire had broken out shortly after asking his passenger to help him fill the car with petrol. He had offered the man a cigar, which he was smoking at the time, and the car had caught fire because the hitchhiker had spilled petrol on his clothing. However, when officers told him they had clear proof of arson, Rouse's story changed several times. As the police gathered more evidence, so their suspicions grew, and Rouse was eventually charged with murder.

The trial began in January 1931. Evidence was presented to the jury that Rouse had kept several mistresses, and these had included Jenkins, who had identified the burned-out car. The jury also heard that Rouse had fathered several children outside his marriage. One of the mothers was only fourteen years of age, and another fifteen-year-old girl was claiming child support because she was pregnant with his second child. The trial, which journalists dubbed 'The Blazing Car Murder', was widely publicised and more claims of paternity soon emerged from numerous women. The prosecution case was that Rouse had attempted to fake his own death to avoid payment of child support and, in doing so, had killed an innocent homeless man. The jury found him guilty of murder and he was sentenced to death by hanging.

Before his execution, Rouse wrote to a newspaper and made a full confession. He had taken out a life insurance plan for £1,000 which would benefit his wife in the case of his accidental death and then sought out a man roughly the same size and build as him. When he found a lone drunk in a pub called the Swan and Pyramid, Rouse plied him with whisky and, offering to help him find work, took him on a supposed trip to Leicester. Stopping on a quiet country road in the small hours, he had bludgeoned him with a hammer and then set the car alight.

The homeless man was buried in St Edmunds Church under the small cross which was paid for and erected by the shocked villagers of Hardingstone. A metal box containing several newspaper accounts of Rouse's trial was buried with the victim and a new cross was erected above the grave in August 2022. Despite recent DNA testing, his identity remains, to this day, unknown.

14 The 'Canonical Five'

In the late 1880s, terror gripped London's Whitechapel. The most impoverished part of the city was being stalked by a predatory monster who, despite never being caught, became the most infamous serial killer in history. Jack The Ripper, so named for the ferocity of his murders, preyed on lone female sex workers.

The East End was a desperately poor part of the city and murders were already commonplace there. Eleven women were found dead during April to December 1888, but only five have been attributed to the Ripper. The 'Canonical Five', as they are referred to, are all buried in cemeteries around East London and some of the women, although destitute when they were killed, have graves commissioned by the local council via donations from those who were appalled — not only by the murders — but also the heart-breaking lives these women lived before their deaths.

The first victim attributed to Jack the Ripper was Mary Ann Nichols. Known locally as Polly, her mutilated body was found in Bucks Row, Whitechapel. Nichols had taken up work as a prostitute after her husband left her and she relocated to London with their four children. She was a heavy drinker, and her alcoholism nay have been the reason her husband departed. On the evening of 30 August 1880, the night before she was killed, witnesses had seen Nichols staggering around Osborn Street, in Whitechapel, noticeably drunk. At one stage she was seen slumped against the wall of a local greengrocer. A friend of hers later told police that Nichols had spent her rent money several times over that evening on liquor.

The body of Mary Nichols was found by two local men, who were on their way to work at 3.40 am. She had clearly been murdered and her throat had been slashed. Her funeral was held on 6 September 1888, and she was buried in the City of London Cemetery in Manor Park, E15. The slaying had shocked all London and thousands of mourners lined the streets to witness the funeral cortège, including Nichol's estranged husband and two of their children. There is no grave or headstone for Mary but, in 2017, a plaque was installed with her name to mark the spot where she was buried, and visitors often leave pennies and flowers on the plaque as a gesture to the woman who became famous for all the wrong reasons. Nor was hers to be the last brutal killing in the district.

Nichols had been pronounced dead by a local physician, Dr Lewellen. He later performed a full autopsy on her, and his findings have since been extensively documented in books and film. On a visit to Tower Hamlets Cemetery, last summer, while wandering through the maze of graves and carefully stepping over strangling ivy and overgrown wildflowers, I found the grave of Dr Lewellyn himself, often referred to as 'The Jack The Ripper Doctor'. It towers over other headstones in the cemetery and is often the first grave a local historian or guide will mention. Lewellyn died in 1921 and his grave is still one of the most notable in the cemetery. The imposing family monument, with an urn and drapery design, can be found close to the main gate of Tower Hamlets Cemetery and local volunteers regularly point it out.

Dr Lewellyn likely contributed a lot more to the medical world than an autopsy on a murder victim but, due to the notoriety of the crimes and the mystery behind the elusive killer, he is linked for eternity to the killings and the story. Despite the brutality of the murder, and with police on high alert, just eight days later in the same area, Annie Chapman was found dead by an elderly resident in Hanbury Street, Whitechapel. Her throat had been cut and her body mutilated. Chapman, who was known to have worked as a flower seller and casual prostitute, is buried in Manor Park Cemetery, East London and a small sign has been erected by the local council to show an approximate location for where she was interred.

The Metropolitan Police were under increasing pressure to capture the killer. Alarm spread across the East End and lurid newspapers accounts stoked further fear. Nevertheless, despite the public outcry and police being on full alert, the Ripper struck again and took the life of another prostitute called, Elizabeth Stride. Known locally as 'Long Liz' as she was tall and lean, the third murder was the only one where mutilation did not occur. Stride was found by a local man, Louis Diemschultz, who had entered Dutfields Yard, Whitechapel, with his horse and cart. His horse abruptly veered to the left when Diemschutz saw a dark object lying on the ground. Lighting a match, he could see that it was the body of a woman who still had blood flowing from a deep wound in her neck.

As police began to investigate the Stride murder, another hideously mutilated body was found in Whitechapel. Catherine Eddows had been mutilated beyond recognition, and her killer had even removed part of her kidney and taken it with him when he left the scene.

Police received an anonymous letter from someone claiming to be the killer, but it proved to be a hoax. It would be the first of many letters written by fantasists, taunting and mocking the police for not solving the mystery or capturing the killer. Jack's fifth victim was Mary Kelly whose grave can be found in St Patricks Cemetery in Leytonstone. Her mutilated corpse was discovered in a slum frequented by prostitutes and criminals on Dorset Street, Spitalfields, in Whitechapel. Her left arm had been hacked away and partially removed, with the remnants displayed on the bed. Both of her breasts had been removed and her abdominal cavity was empty. Her heart was missing, and her neck had been severed with such ferocity it was almost cut to the spine. Her nose, lips, and eyelids had been hacked away and her dismembered organs and many other body parts were haphazardly strewn across the room.

Mary Jane Kelly's funeral was paid for entirely by a private donor, clearly appalled by the young woman's murder. Visitors to her grave to this day leave gifts: flowers, rosary beads, and miniature bottles of gin. Kelly is also thought to be the ripper's last victim, but other similar murders have been documented after 1888 and some well into the 1890s.

The murders sent shockwaves through the community and thousands lined the streets in support of Jack's victims. No one was ever caught or charged for any of the killings, but there has been speculation linked to a large number of men over the years. One prime suspect was Thomas Cutbush. I stumbled across a photo of his grave online, and simply had to go and see it for myself. His gravestone is almost completely covered by invasive ivy and is located in a crumbling part of Nunhead Cemetery, in London. As I made my way through the graveyard it was easy to get lost but, armed with a photo and a few pointers from an on-site volunteer, I found the ageing tombstone — guarded by a closely situated angel — which topped another grave.

Cutbush was born in 1866 making him just 22 when the murders occurred. It is alleged that he had a hatred of women, particularly prostitutes, as he believed he had contracted syphilis by paying for sex. He displayed behavioural problems from a young age and was even dismissed from his job, having pushed his boss down a flight of stairs. He was said to have had a keen interest in medicine and studied books on the subject religiously. Cutbush was never charged for assaulting his boss, nor was he questioned by police for the 1888 killings but, in 1891, he was convicted of stabbing two Whitechapel women in the buttocks and committed indefinitely to Broadmoor psychiatric hospital.

At various times more than one hundred men have been suspected of being the nefarious Jack The Ripper, but his true identity remains a mystery. In an era when violent death was commonplace, the killings of 1888 still managed to shock the world and continue to intrigue historians to this day. Jack the Ripper remains the most notorious serial killer of all time, over 125 years after his crimes.

15 Funeral circus

As technology evolves and our world becomes more interconnected, the need to share our daily lives with others grows, and there are some who try and interact with others beyond the grave. I recently heard of a man who was able to plan for his funeral knowing that he had been diagnosed with a form of terminal cancer. Shay Bradley — a lifelong wag — was a war veteran from Dublin who died from colon cancer, following a three-year battle. Joking with his family one day, he came up with a macabre but ingenious prank which he plotted with his son.

To give the mourners one last laugh, a pre-recorded message would be played from inside his coffin. The funeral took place at Bohernabreena Cemetery, Kilkenny, Ireland and, at the very moment the coffin was committed to the ground, the message was clearly heard by those gathered around the graveside. As stunned family members fought back tears Bradley could be heard knocking on the coffin lid and shouting, 'Let me out, it's fucking dark in here! Where the fuck am I? Is that a priest I can hear? This is Shay, I'm in the box!'

Shay's son, Jonathan, recorded the prank with Bradley's family laughing and comforting one another as they looked on in disbelief. The video was posted online, and it quickly went viral. Johnathan was interviewed by newspapers and said that his father was, 'A larger-than-life character who always wanted to make people laugh. He wanted something special and for everyone to remember him as he used to be, so that everyone, especially my mother, did not leave the graveside sombre.'

Bradley made his family smile but also, inadvertently, inspired the entire world as 'Shay's last laugh' became a worldwide media storm. This was an ingenious practical joke, but the concept of including something interactive for mourners is becoming popular. Funerals can now be livestreamed for family members who cannot attend the service. Recordings can be passed on to others or sent via an online link.

A funeral director in Poole, Dorset offers customers the option of having QR codes inscribed onto a person's headstone. The codes can then be scanned using a mobile phone which will take visitors to a webpage where they can read more about a deceased person and can even leave messages of condolence for the family. The family has access to the webpage via a password and log in anytime where they can freely upload information about a person who has passed away and read the messages left by mourners.

A company in Slovenia offers barcoded gravestones and has even installed large television screens in some cemeteries, which play videos of the deceased at the touch of a button. The TV screens are weatherproof, as well as vandal-proof and the company is hoping to develop the screens so that the sound can be discretely played via a mobile phone and listened to using headphones. Elsewhere in the world solar-powered plaques, lighting, and even jukeboxes are appearing in graveyards.

I have to admit that part of what drives me to seek out an unusual grave or tomb is the intrigue of being able to unravel the past. I absolutely adore researching a person's grave and finding that person's story, through archives and books. Oftentimes a gravestone only shows the deceased's name and date of birth and death. If that person was well known, wealthy, or a member of royalty it can be relatively easy to find out more about them via the Internet, but the challenge is greater for ordinary folk.

On a recent visit to Kensal Rise Cemetery, as I meandered through the jam-packed graves with my uncle Pat as my guide, he gave me a useful tip. There are over 65,000 graves in Kensal Green and Pat explained how to use markers to locate our family graves, 'the only way to find them amongst all these poor souls.'

As we weaved through the many tombs, graves, and monuments, Pat told me to look out for the statue of a man boxing. I wasn't sure if he was joking but, treading carefully and apologising to the dead as I stepped on their final resting places, I finally came upon a crudely made miniature statue of a man boxing, complete with red and white shorts and bright red boxing gloves. He was frozen in a boxing stance and standing proudly over the grave of a Romany gypsy man.

Kensal Green is segregated into several areas and my family resides in the so-called 'Catholic section', along with many others of mainly Irish, Italian, and Romany descent. The boxing man statue was placed just a few metres from where my great aunt Dina and her son Gerald are buried. My paternal grandparents are also buried nearby but in another section of the cemetery and we didn't have an unusual statue to help locate their grave. I had to rely on Pat who told me to 'look for a black gravestone'. There were quite a few, so I followed quietly behind and placed a single red rose on my grandparent's grave when we found it. Then I emptied the font of stagnant water and cleaned the leaves from the ground where the wind had blown debris onto the plot.

It was a sad moment to finally see the grave of my grandparents. I had never met my grandmother; she passed away from peritonitis following surgery when my father was five and my uncle Pat just 3. We had moved to Bournemouth a few years before my paternal grandfather passed from a heart attack in the early 1980s, so I did not know either of my paternal grandparents. Nonetheless, as I stood over the grave, which had subsided causing the headstone to list, I couldn't help but wonder if they might be able to see what we were doing. Would they know that we had lovingly cleaned the gravesite? Could they see how tenderly Pat and I looked on?

It was at that moment that I realised what a headstone is really for. It is a marker for those who love you, who need to visit your resting place, stop for a moment and hold you in their hearts. A monument is so much more about those that are left behind than the person who has passed. The 'boxing man' statue certainly did help locate my great aunt's grave, and I am sure I can easily locate it again.

The 'boxing man' wasn't the only unusual grave marker in this area of the cemetery. I came across a grave with two life-size statues of a husband and wife proudly standing guard together over another family plot. The graveyard is huge and some of the most elaborate graves in the Catholic area belong to the graves of Irish Travellers. I have no links to the traveller community by blood, but I did go to school with mainly third- and fourth-generation travellers.

I am fascinated by traveller history, their devotion to God, and the traditions that surround the community. Their tight-knit values make it hard to discover how they celebrate life and death, and the community can be impenetrable to outsiders. Death and the afterlife can be a taboo subject among travellers, despite their stereotypical portrayal as tarot and tea leaf readers. However, the tombs, gravestones, and memorials of those once loved by the traveller community are often large, imposing, sombre, and beautiful. Some traveller graves can be garish and over-elaborate, even brutalist. But I smile when I see one as they have always been recently visited and gifts such as money, cards, unopened cans of larger, and mementoes have been left by family members.

One traveller grave that has ruffled a few feathers recently is that of a man called Willy Collins who, in life, was a champion bare-knuckle boxer known as 'The Big Willy' and 'The King of Sheffield'. Willy sadly passed while away on holiday in Mallorca aged just 49. He was supposed to be celebrating his wife's birthday but collapsed suddenly and died, breaking the hearts of all who loved him. A post-mortem examination revealed that Collins had suffered a haemorrhage brought on by complications of a stomach ulcer he had been battling.

Collins met his wife when she was just 11 years old, and they married as soon as she turned 17. His family planned and built an enormous tombstone which was erected in Shiregreen Cemetery. It has been called a monstrosity by some and there have been requests from many for it to be demolished. Sheffield council has confirmed that the marble tomb, weighing a whopping 37 tons, was erected without planning permission, a fact that the Collins family vehemently disputes. However, the size and weight of the memorial are not the main reason for all of the fuss. The gargantuan tombstone, which includes two life-size carvings of Mr Collins, several biblical sculptures, and four twelve-foot-high flag poles flying the Irish flag, has been installed with LED lights and a solar-powered jukebox that plays Willy's favourite songs. Two marble gates lead into the memorial which spreads across a large patch of grass and there is a hefty marble carved bench engraved with the word King in gold leaf.

Photos of the extraordinary monument began circulating on the Internet almost as soon as it was completed, and the story of the elaborate grave was featured in many newspapers. Thousands lined the streets to see his gold-plated coffin make its way to church, and then to the cemetery.

Collins' family claim that the council signed off the plans and feel that they have been discriminated against in an act of blatant racism. However, many locals believe that Collins' grave is disrespectful to others buried in the cemetery with some families claiming that their requests for items as small as picket fences were refused by the council. Whatever the council finally decides they are bound to offend someone. Meanwhile, Collins' gigantic tomb continues to dominate the graveyard.

Another traveller grave that has attracted attention for well over one hundred years is that of Corlinda Lee in Glasgow's Necropolis. This fascinating cemetery is Glasgow's grandest and is often referred to as the 'City of the dead'. Visitors flock to the burial site including celebrities. Miley Cyrus, Hugh Jackman and others have recently been spotted. Necropolis was built after the cathedral cemetery — which sits just across the road — became full and a new site was needed. Stonemasons here have carved out designs for the dead by well-known artists such as Rennie Mackintosh and Alexander 'Greek' Thomson.

Corlinda Lee's tomb attracts a lot of attention and well-wishers often leave coins that they force into the joints of the stonework. Corlinda was a Romany gypsy who was born into a prominent gypsy family, based in Epping, Essex. The Lees were part of a close-knit community and in 1865, when Corlinda married horse trainer George Smith — a member of another prominent gypsy family — she linked two important dynasties, and they became something of a power couple. George, who was born under the surname Buckley but changed it to his mother's maiden name after his father was killed in a pub brawl, eventually became the clan chief of ten Gypsy families, a coveted and respected role within the community. This rise in status secured George and Corlinda as King and Queen of the Gypsies. They had eight children and toured the country with other families, under George's careful direction, giving non-gypsies an insight into the lives of the travellers. George marketed these events as 'Gypsy Balls' and, as the Victorians were intrigued by anything unusual or mysterious, the great tours were a huge success. George was a vibrant character but shrewd when it came to money. Members of the public could come and see how Gypsy Travellers lived, view their caravans, and talk about the horses they kept, while the ladies could enjoy having their palms read. Corlinda was known for her exceptional crystal ball readings, all for a small fee of course. Crossing Corlinda's palm with silver would ensure that she would reveal your future.

There was huge interest in the paranormal, especially mediumship and the spirit world, in Victorian England. George's marketing must have worked because it was during one ball, which was held at Knockenhair Park in Dunbar, that Queen Victoria had her palm read by Corlinda. The Queen recorded the reading in her diary which secured Corlinda's reputation, and the family dined off the story for years. But the family's good fortune didn't last forever and when George Smith fell into financial difficulties he was reported to have died. A few months later he was spotted walking around a small village in South Wales, and it is rumoured that he benefited from a fraudulent life insurance claim. When he finally did pass away, he was buried next to Corlinda in Glasgow's Necropolis.

Corlinda's tombstone was designed and made by one of Glasgow's foremost monumental masons, Robert Gray. A portrait of her was cast in bronze and mounted on the tombstone, but it was stolen, and a plaster replica later replaced it. The inscription on the stone reads:

GRAVE CONCERNS

CORLINDA LEE
Queen of the Gipsies
Beloved wife of George Smith
Who died at 42 New City Road, Glasgow, on 28
March 1900, aged 68 years and lies here beside her
beloved son Ernest
Her love for her children was great and she was
charitable to the poor. Wherever she pitched her
tent she was loved and respected by all.
Her grandchild baby May
Given 17th May 1897
Taken 14th July 1898

The 'Singing Grave' of a famous clown, Joseph Grimaldi, can be found in the public park named after the actor, just off Pentonville Road, North London. Grimaldi was an English entertainer, born into a family of Italian immigrants in London, on 18 December 1778. His parents were performers and little Joseph made his debut appearance on stage at Drury Lane, alongside his father, aged just two. Grimaldi quickly established himself as a child performer and went on to adapt his comedy skills to curate and develop a clown act so successful that it became the blueprint for all clowns from the early 1780s onwards.

His signature white face makeup and highly energetic, comedic performances are still used today, and clowns are often referred to within the industry as 'Joeys'. Grimaldi was London's most famous clown act, having starred at Sadlers Wells Theatre and Covent Garden (at one point, simultaneously). Tragically, Grimaldi ended his days battling alcoholism and depression. He died in poverty at the age of just 58. His grave, which can be found within the North London park, attracts clowns from all over the world, mostly on the anniversary of his passing. Since the 1940s an annual memorial service has been held on the first Sunday in February at Holy Trinity Church in Hackney. It attracts hundreds of clown performers from all over the world who often attend the service in full clown costume.

In 2010, a local artist made Grimaldi's grave interactive. Henry Krokatsis was commissioned to install something 'different' within the park. He designed two coffin-shaped structures made up of musical tiles that, when stepped or danced on, create different musical sounds. By selecting the right tiles, it is possible for visitors to play the tune of *Hot Coddlins*, Grimaldi's most famous song. The lyrics tell of a woman who sold baked apples on the streets of London and spent the money on gin.

Grimaldi's original grave is untouched, and the coffin-shaped musical keyboards are found on the grass to one side of the park. His is a traditionally styled headstone which, at some point in time, has been fenced off with iron railings. They feature the traditional comedy and tragedy masks — synonymous with the performing arts' world — cast in iron and mounted on the front of the fence. Joseph left such a powerful legacy that he is still known in the theatre world as 'the King of Clowns'. The interactive installation on his grave is called *An Invitation To Dance On The Grave*.

16 Myths & martyrs

I t was Benjamin Franklin who said 'there are only two things certain in life; death and taxes', and it is true that we all succumb to the sands of time at some point. What to do with our mortal remains then becomes an issue for those we leave behind. Graveyards are widely spread across the British Isles, and the more of them I find, the more deeply engrossed in history and anthropology I become. It is easy to research some of Britain's best-known graveyards and articles about famous inhabitants are in abundance, particularly on the Internet. Stories of supposed ghost encounters, articles with photographs of unusual tombs, and heart-wrenching graves of those who died in the two world wars, are in abundance, particularly in densely populated parts of the country. However, there are many smaller graveyards, some of which may, at one time, have been part of a larger cemetery which has been divided to make for way for other developments.

Graveyards have always had a sanitary purpose as well as a spiritual one. Early man realised that there was a need to bury their dead, or cremate a corpse, to keep predators at bay and disease away from the living. Thanks to some of the larger cemeteries, such as the Magnificent Seven, our water supply and the areas we inhabit are relatively disease-free. However, burying a person quickly for sanitary reasons has often resulted in burials away from family and, sometimes, without anyone familiar to mourn their passing.

Through my unusual hobby of tombstone tourism, I often find tales of people who passed away far from home and were buried where they died. Most of the graves I researched had links to the two world wars. Stories of crashed pilots buried in mountain ranges, or remote areas, having been shot down by the enemy, were fairly common. One story, in particular, made me question if a man's death could have been avoided.

A E Wall was the Chief Stoker aboard HMS *Curacoa*. His work, deep in the bowels of the ship, was hot, dirty and dangerous. As well as stoking the furnaces he would also have been required to maintain the boilers, which meant climbing inside to clean and repair them. Originally built in 1919 as a C-Class light cruiser for the Royal Navy, *Curacoa* was launched too late to see action in World War One, but spent most of her time escorting convoys of merchant ships during World War Two.

On 2 October 1942, HMS *Curacoa* was accompanying the legendary Cunard liner, RMS *Queen Mary*, north of Ireland, when the captains of the two ships misinterpreted each other's courses. The resulting collision led to 337 of the ship's crew ending their days at the bottom of the cold Irish Sea. The *Queen Mary* struck the side of her escort ship with such force that she cut the cruiser in half.

A E Wall's body washed ashore in Scotland a few days after the disaster. He was just 42 years of age, and he was buried without any family members present to offer prayers or to mourn his passing. Because of the danger of U-Boats, the *Queen Mary* could not stop to rescue the drowning men. She steamed on ahead and radioed for help. 101 men were eventually pulled from the sea, but only some of them went on to survive. There is a memorial for the lost seamen at the Chatham Naval Museum. Some of the victims were buried in Chatham and others in Arisaig

Cemetery, in Inverness-shire, but A E Wall was buried in Kilchoan Cemetery, simply because his body washed up close to its shore.

Kilchoan is an ancient burial site, and some of its graves are believed to be Viking, but it is not Britain's oldest cemetery. Aveline's Hole, which rests on a narrow gorge on the outskirts of Somerset, has that distinction, and scientists believe that it may have been used more than ten thousand years ago, just after the last Ice Age. Ancient bones have been found in the location and it is believed that its crematorium was abandoned around six thousand years ago — a time when the first stones of the Egyptian pyramids were being laid.

The earliest tomb at Aveline's Hole was discovered in the late 1700s by two young schoolboys who were out rabbit poaching. They stumbled on a crack in the gorge and, peering inside, found a cave packed to the roof with human skeletons. As news spread, archaeologists, many of them amateurs, flocked to the area and accidentally desecrated much of what had been discovered. The remainder of the bones and fragments of early man were saved and eventually found a home at Bristol University, but when the building was bombed, in World War Two, much of the collection was lost. Today, just a few fragments remain in museum collections across the country.

For me, the older and more fragmented a cemetery is, the better. Although I enjoy war cemeteries, with their clean lines of tombstones in uniform positions. I also love weaving my way through an unkempt cemetery with crumbling earth, broken pathways, lichen-covered walls, and sunken tombs. I can see beauty in the decay and disorder of an old churchyard. So much life can be found in a place where death seems like the only focus.

Death is often called the final frontier, but there is always life in a graveyard, whether it be family members visiting their loved ones' graves, flowers erupting out of tarmac pathways, or birds nesting in the rubbish left behind by others. I once witnessed a magpie carrying half a coconut shell as it flew low through a cemetery in North London. The shell became too heavy for the bird but, no sooner had it fallen from its beak, than a squirrel collected the shell and took it into a tree. Not only are graveyards places of reflection, where one can ponder one's own mortality, but they are usually a haven for wildlife; an enchanted place to spot birdlife and small mammals.

The arrival of a lone robin in a cemetery is said to symbolise a loved one coming back from the spirit world to visit a person who is mourning, and they can almost always be found sat on top of a headstone or fence post. The sudden appearance of a black cat in a cemetery has been an old wives' tale for centuries, associated across the world with bad luck or ill health. Seeing a black cat in a cemetery is not thought to be a good omen and when one sidled up against me on a visit to York Cemetery, I wondered if perhaps I was being followed by what is known as a witch's familiar. A familiar is said to be a magical demon, genie, or imp posing in the form of an animal to run errands or do evil deeds for its witchy master. The black feline that followed me around York Cemetery did seem to appear from out of nowhere. He or she then continued to follow my daughter and me for several minutes, before seemingly disappearing, most likely around a corner or headstone. Of course, a more logical but less intriguing explanation for the appearance of the cat may have been the headless rat carcasses that lay on the ground. Vermin thrive in almost every cemetery. Catching a small snack is easy for a cat, especially in a quiet area when the footfall of humans is low and there is an abundance of hollow hideouts to stake out unsuspecting prey.

Cemeteries offer a plethora of other things to research, apart from the lives of their inhabitants and old wives' tales. Among the strangling ivy found growing in almost every cemetery, are interesting and beautiful plants which can be seen in every corner of a churchyard. I recently discovered a beautiful little flower growing out of the crack in a wall of one of the main gates to Nunhead cemetery. Its invitingly deep purple, star-shaped petals made me question what the plant might be, and if it had been deliberately planted there. Flowers have been used in burials for centuries, not just to commemorate a person's passing, but often to ward off evil. The purple bloom had me guessing and I wondered if it may be a flower or a weed, as oftentimes the most common invasive weeds have the prettiest of flowers.

Bindweed, also known as Granny Pop Out of Bed, is another common wildflower found in cemeteries and a plant that always brings a smile to my face when I see it. My siblings and I would have hours of fun chasing one another with some of the white trumpet-like flowers, which can be popped out with your fingers, as we tried to ping a flower onto one another's heads. In search of the answer to the origins of the mystery of the star-shaped plant, I did what any good researcher does, and used the Internet. An app I recently downloaded quickly identified the plant and took me to a webpage that gave me its name and origins. I was amazed to learn that the purple flower was not a native species but something that was likely planted by a human. It was called the Serbian Bellflower: a semi-evergreen, it is native to the Dinaric Alps of former Yugoslavia. The plant is purely ornamental and is often buried at gravesites by mourners as it is said to promote hope, longevity, and everlasting love.

Tower Hamlets Cemetery unleashed a heady mix of floral scents when I visited last summer. Volunteers have planted herbs, bulbs, flowers, and shrubs — a common way for councils to affordably spruce up an ageing graveyard. In the 1980s, Tower Hamlets Cemetery was all but derelict. Today it has a café, arts and crafts classes, and other money-making events which help to conserve the 27 acres of cemetery land. While it is still free to enter this cemetery, others, including Highgate, charge an entrance fee to visitors. Photography, however, is now banned within the grounds of the majority of cemeteries.

Highgate Cemetery relies heavily on visitor fees and the opportunity to donate is also signposted and encouraged. Today, virtually all cemeteries, whatever the style of the tombs and monuments or the state of the land around them, encourage curious visitors like me, as well as photographers from all over the world looking for the perfect shot for their online blogs or social media accounts.

The Martyrs Grave, which can be found in the grounds of The Valley Cemetery, Stirling, Scotland, is highly unusual and top of the bucket list for amateur and professional photographers. The striking white marble and glass dome-shaped tomb can be easily found within the grounds of the churchyard and holds the remains of two sisters called Margaret and Agnes Wilson, aged 18 and 13 respectively. The sisters, along with an elderly neighbour, were sentenced to death by hanging in 1685. The trio were devout Covenanters and firmly believed in their Presbyterian faith, a sect strongly opposed by the monarchy who wanted to impose an English-style Anglican form of worship.

Covenanters continued to practice their faith despite the risk of being put to death. They had been forced out of their churches and could only worship in small outdoor gatherings or clandestine ceremonies in the hills. In 1660 the Covenanter's Presbyterian faith was declared treasonable and by 1684 their secret gatherings became even riskier. If caught by the authorities, followers were ordered to recount their faith and show allegiance to the King or face death. Margaret had been attending secret meetings with her brother Thomas for some time and on occasion, they brought along their little sister Agnes, but one afternoon in February 1685 the two girls went to a secret prayer meeting in Wigtown with an elderly widow called Margaret McLachlan. The military presence was high that day and the three women were caught, questioned on the spot and, after refusing to drink to the King's health, they were thrown into prison. A few days later they were taken to the assizes in Wigtownshire.

Accused of high reason, the trio were asked to renounce their faith or face the death penalty, a common order at the time. All three women refused and, despite a campaign for clemency by the sister's father, Gilbert Wilson, the girls and their neighbour, Margaret MacLauchlan, were sentenced to death by hanging. Gilbert Wilson continued to campaign for his daughters and managed to buy his youngest daughter's freedom for 100 Scottish pounds, but her older sister Margaret and Mrs Mclaughlin were not so lucky. Although the two women were granted a reprieve by the Privy Council of Scotland, it was either ignored or never reached the court. Wilson and 60-year-old McLaughlin were taken to Solway Firth where they were chained to wooden stakes and left to drown at high tide.

The monument that stands today was erected sometime after the executions. Many believe that the glass dome with its cobalt blue glass and top panels referencing Christ, was installed to stop the spirits of the women from escaping from the tomb. The women became martyrs of their faith, revered for centuries and the brilliant white tomb is often referred to as The Wigtown Martyrs Monument.

I heard a similarly harrowing story when filming on location in Guernsey a few years back. There is no grave to visit for Peretine Massey, her sister Guillemin Gilbert and their mother Catherine Cawches, but there is a plaque on a wall close to the place where these three women met with a horrific death. The three had been accused of stealing a golden goblet in 1556 by a man called Vincent Gossett. At the time, Perotine was married to a Calvinist minister, but he had left the island and moved to London, most likely to escape persecution.

These were dangerous times for Protestants. During her five-year reign, Queen Mary, also known as 'Bloody Mary', had over 280 religious dissenters burned at the stake during the Marian persecutions. At their trial, all three women were found not guilty when their accuser, Vincent Gossett, admitted that he had lied about the theft of the goblet. Gossett was ordered to have his ear nailed to a pillory, but the three women faced further charges. It had been noted during their trial that the women had not been attending church in an era when this was considered sacrilege. They were charged with heresy and imprisoned in the notorious Castle Cornet. Perotine, who was pregnant at the time, claimed that the women had been attending mass, but their neighbours disagreed, and all three women were condemned to be burned at the stake.

In the past, pregnant women had been spared from being burned alive, but during Mary's reign no such mercy was shown. Perotine, her sister, and their mother were tied to wooden stakes on 18 July 1556 and a fire lit at their feet. The women should have been strangled by the executioner to spare them the agony of the flames, but the rope broke, and the women were burned alive. Perotine was heavily pregnant and screamed before she fell unconscious in the flames. Her swollen belly burst open, and her foetus fell out into the fire. A man called William House rescued the tiny baby, a boy, and laid him on a patch of grass. Several women ran to help the child but the chief executioner, Helier Gosselin, ordered that the baby be cast back into the flames. The innocent child met the same fate as his mother, aunt, and grandmother.

Guernsey had become known as 'the witch-hunting capital of Europe' for many similar acts against heretics and so-called witches. However, the execution of Perotine Massey, her child, Guilomine Gilbert, and Katherine

Cawches was to be the last of its kind. Bloody Mary's reign came to an end when she died of what is suspected to have been a ruptured ovarian cyst or uterine cancer. In the weeks leading up to her death, Mary had assumed that she was with child, but she passed away on 17 November 1558 aged 42 and no child was found within her womb. She is buried in Westminster Abbey.

When Mary Tudor's sister, Elizabeth, took the throne, many Protestants accused of heresy were still awaiting execution. Guernaise locals campaigned for Helier Gosselin to be tried for the murder of the baby boy. Elizabeth, however, decided to pardon him along with 283 other people who had taken part in the burning of Protestants during her sister's reign. A plaque for the three women was commissioned and placed close to the execution site in the town of St Peter Port. Their story is often confused with the many witch trials which took place on the island, but this harrowing tale was simply a story of three women, in the wrong place at the wrong time, under the rule of one of Britain's most ruthless queens.

The last witch trial on the island of Guernsey occurred as recently as 1914. A woman called Aimee Lake was accused of being a witch after trying to extort money from one of her customers. Lake had become known for telling fortunes and reading the tea leaves on the island, but she found herself in hot water when she was accused of putting a curse on one of her neighbours. Lake had earned a modest income in her career as a psychic and, although she claimed not to charge for her services, she did both encourage and accept donations. She was also said to have offered spells for those in need and often gave rings or charms to her clients and sold powders to ward off evil or bring about good fortune.

She was accused of extortion by a neighbour, Mrs Houtin, who said that Lake had put a curse on her and demanded £3 for its removal, failing which Houtin would die. Witchcraft was still feared by many people, even after the turn of the century, and Houtin was said to be living in terror. She became a recluse, only opening the door when she was sure police were there to take her statement.

Lake was brought before a court and charged. Police had found charms, powders, and pagan paraphernalia in her home and she was convicted of witchcraft and sentenced to eight days in prison. She was lucky, you might say, given that so many other 'witches' of the past had been brutally executed. Today, Aimee Lake would likely have been let off with a caution, but she became the last person to be accused, charged and convicted of witchcraft on the Island of Guernsey.

Aimee Lake, pictured with her husband and children, was the last person on the Island of Guernsey to be accused, charged and convicted of witchcraft.

17 Tombs fit for a king

A stone's throw from my home is a monument that has had me guessing since I moved to the area almost two decades ago. A stone pyramid sits in St Anne's Churchyard and is known locally as The Limehouse Pyramid. This mysterious piece of architecture, which is not (as far as we know) a tomb or gravestone, has intrigued people for many years and is even featured in Sax Rohmer's crime stories, *The Mystery of Dr Fu-Manchu*, first published in 1913. Limehouse was home to a small but closely knit Chinese community in the late 1880s and many of the streets around the area show nods to the Orient, including road names such as Ming Street, Canton Street, and Pekin Street all of which surround the churchyard of St Anne's.

Well-established plum trees can be found growing in abundance in the area. They are thought to have been planted to create oriental plum sauce and are often found alongside tall fronds of bamboo. Limehouse made the perfect setting for Rohmer's stories in which The Limehouse Pyramid became the entrance to the evil doctor's opium den. Fu Manchu means long, straight moustache in Chinese, and a 1965 film starring Sir Christopher Lee as the evil doctor has become a minor classic.

There is a theory that the pyramid was originally meant to sit on top of the church, but it is unlikely we will ever know for certain. It is made of Portland stone and would, originally, have been sparkling white, but is now grey and covered in lichen. It also bears a coat of arms with the inscription 'The Wisdom Of Solomon', leading many to think the curious structure has links to Freemasons. Designer Nicholas Hawksmoor was often referred to as 'the Devil's Architect' and was also a noted Freemason. His buildings often displayed 'pagan' symbols as well as Egyptian ideograms and obelisks.

Each of the four sides of the pyramid is divided into five horizontal segments. In Freemasonry, five is a sacred number because it is formed by the union of the first even and the first odd number, rejecting unity and symbolising the mixed conditions of order and disorder, happiness and misfortune, life and death. In Egypt, the five major planets and the five elementary powers were considered sacred. Perhaps only Hawksmoor knows why the pyramid resides where it does and maybe he departed this world taking the mystery to the grave with him.

Another grave in St Anne's churchyard is known locally as the 'upside-down-right-way-up' headstone. Edward Foorde's grave has the same inscription on both the back and front of the stone, but one side of the text has to be read upside down. It is an intriguing and fun headstone and sits just a few rows away from the curious pyramid. Weathered with time, the gravestone has suffered damage to the side that reads upside down, but still makes for a good photo opportunity, and is certainly one to visit when navigating the churchyard. Whatever the Limehouse pyramid was, or is, these wonderful monuments will undoubtedly keep people guessing for generations to come.

Pyramid-shaped tombs are found all over the country and many are the subject of myth and local legend. One spectacular pyramid in Brightling, Suffolk, stands in a dark and moody corner of St Thomas Beckett Churchyard. Photographs often show the monument surrounded by sheep of the Suffolk variety gently nibbling away at the surrounding grass. The sheep seem to care nothing for the imposing structure which has been in place for several centuries and was erected to house the body of a John Fuller. Earning the nickname 'Mad Jack Fuller' he came from a wealthy family and served as Member of Parliament for Southampton and Sussex. The Fuller family had made their fortune from the iron trade. When Mad Jack's uncle died in 1777, he received a large portion of his estate including several slave plantations in Jamaica. Aged just 20 when he inherited, Mad Jack was young, rich, and moving in powerful circles. Unfortunately, he was also a heavy drinker, and his temper frequently got the better of him.

He was ejected from parliament in 1810 after a public drunken rant in which he railed against the British government. So serious was his outburst that he risked imprisonment in the Tower of London. He managed to escape jail, but never lost his reputation as an outspoken drunkard. Mad Jack did, however, spend some of his wealth on other interests and was deeply intrigued by science. Among others, he mentored Michael Faraday, financing his studies into electricity and other pioneering scientific experiments.

Mad Jack also had a keen interest in the ancient world, and he planned his own Egyptian-style mausoleum long before he departed the earth. Work began on his funeral pyramid around 1810, twenty-four years before his death in 1834. After his death there were rumours that he was interred within the tomb, above the ground in a seated position on an iron chair, dressed in a suit and top hat. It was even believed that the tomb contained a table, set with roasted chicken, and a bottle of port, and broken glass was scattered on the floor to prick the feet of the Devil, if he tried to enter.

These rumours were quashed in 1982 when restoration work began. They involved extensive repairs to the inside of the pyramid, but workmen found no corpse, no table and no broken glass. All the same, I relish rumours like Fuller's, they can last for centuries if not disproved by an expert or investigator. I can only imagine the minds of those visiting the churchyard when Jack was interred; people must have been scared out of their wits walking past an imposing tomb with such a sinister story.

However, the story of a man sitting upright, waiting for the devil to arrive was not limited to Mad Jack Fuller. Another pyramid-shaped tomb in St Andrew's Presbyterian Churchyard, in Rodney Street, Liverpool, offers a strikingly similar but far more disturbing story than Fuller's. The three-sided tomb belongs to a man called William Mackenzie, a former weaver's assistant and civil engineer, who died in 1851. Mackenzie had worked on some of Europe's most important railways and canals and become moderately wealthy. However, according to legend, he was also a compulsive gambler who lost his soul in a game of poker with the Devil himself.

After his death, rumours began to spread that Mackenzie had ordered his body to be placed above ground, as he believed if he was not buried beneath the earth, the devil would not be able to collect his prize. Some alleged that Mackenzie was placed into the pyramid-shaped tomb sitting in an upright position, in a chair, while holding a winning hand of poker cards to further mock the hooved overlord.

Just a few decades after Mackenzie's death, reports of a haunting within the cemetery circulated and many believed that the gambler had not evaded eternal damnation. Several locals had seen a dark shadow lurking in the churchyard. The first sighting was in 1871, when a local resident reported seeing a phantom floating above the graves. After describing a man strikingly similar to Mackenzie but with 'black and lifeless eyes' the witness is alleged to have died of fright! The shadowy phantom, dressed in a top hat and cape, was said to have walked through the locked gates of the graveyard before disappearing into the pyramid. The pyramid still stands in the churchyard on Rodney Street, and it is still thought to be haunted by Mackenzie's ghost, but there have been no recent sightings.

The influence of ancient Egypt can be seen in many cemeteries, but Christian emblems have frequently been added to avoid the appearance of paganism. Cherubs, crosses, and images of Christ are often carved into Egyptian-style monuments, seemingly guarding the tombs of those long departed. Egyptomania had begun in the early 19th century following Napoleon Bonaparte's campaign in Egypt and Syria. France was particularly taken with the monumental designs from Egypt which were popularised by a series of books entitled *Description de l'Égypte*. These were based on notes and drawings completed by Napoleon himself, along with the scientists and scholars who accompanied him and comprehensively catalogued almost everything they encountered along the way. Their findings were compiled into the largest published work in the world. First Paris, and later all Europe, would be mesmerised by the treasures that had been uncovered.

Funerary architecture had been influenced by Egypt before Napoleon's invasion and a handful of structures dating back to the Renaissance period have Egyptian motifs. However, they were often follies rather than tombs or mausoleums. London and Paris have always been synonymous with fashion and the impact of the Egyptian revival can be seen all over graveyards within both cities. Highgate Cemetery, completed in 1839, has a large section called Egyptian Avenue which opens out to a circle of family tombs known as The Circle of Lebanon. The entrance is flanked by two very large obelisks which are proceeded by a huge stone doorway, complete with iron gates and locks which appear to have been purposefully placed, upside down, adding to the mystery and intrigue of the place.

Such was the impact of Egyptomania on the Victorians — who already harboured a deep obsession with death — that parties called 'unwrapping ceremonies' were held in the homes of the wealthy. These involved mummies, some real and some fake, being unwrapped before fascinated guests. In 1828, one family took their obsession with mummification a step further when their relative, Hannah Beswick, passed away. She was a rich woman, born into a wealthy family in Manchester in 1688. Inheriting a substantial fortune when her father died in1706, she moved into a manor house, Birchin Bower, in Hollingwood, Oldham. Here she lived an extravagant and very comfortable life with every luxury that wealth can bring. For all this, however, Hannah was terrified of death: when her brother John was pronounced dead, she saw his eyelids flicker as the undertaker was about to close the coffin lid. A doctor was called who confirmed that John was, indeed, still alive and he recovered, living for many more years.

Comas were not fully understood at the time and misdiagnoses like John's were not uncommon. Hannah developed an all-consuming fear of being buried alive. In her will, which she wrote the year before her death, it stated that her corpse must be kept above ground and checked regularly for signs of life. She also ordered that her funeral only take place if a physician was absolutely sure that she had passed away. She entrusted these duties to her friend and personal physician, Dr Charles White. Obsessed with anatomy, White was alleged to have been the owner of several oddities and curiosities of both the 'wet and dry' variety. It was fashionable at the time for members of the medical profession to collect jars of deformed animals and foetuses. Among White's collection was the skeleton of

Thomas Higgins, a notorious highwayman who had been hanged for his crimes.

Despite no such instruction in her will, White took it upon himself to embalm and mummify Hannah and went on to keep her as part of his collection, stuffing her body into the case of a grandfather clock. This was an age in which the moral boundaries between science and curiosity, education and amusement were far looser than today.

White, who was a founder of the Manchester Royal Infirmary and a pioneer of obstetrics, used a technique known as 'arterial embalming' to preserve Hannah's body. This involved filling the circulatory system with a mixture of turpentine, vermilion, rosemary, and lavender oils. The internal organs were removed, emptied of blood and fluid before being washed with alcohol, and placed back into the body's cavity. He then filled the entire corpse with plaster of Paris before stuffing the openings of the body with camphor and sewing up the skin. Finally, he drenched the cadaver in tar and wrapped the corpse in bandages. The corpse then went on display in White's home. At parties or following requests from visitors, he was known to drag out the makeshift sarcophagus, unveiling the face of Hannah by pulling back a curtain to reveal his handywork.

When White died, the so-called Manchester Mummy was bequeathed to a friend who later donated it to the museum of the Manchester Natural History Society. Placed in the entrance hall, it quickly became the museum's most popular exhibit. As social attitudes changed, however, the Manchester Mummy fell out of favour. On 22 July 1868, Hannah was finally buried in Harpurhey Cemetery, over 110 years after she had died. She lies in an unmarked plot as there were fears such a famous corpse might be a target for graverobbers.

After Hannah's death, a legend grew that her home was haunted by a phantom figure in a black gown and white cap. The ghost would float across the parlour then disappear above a certain flagstone. A resident is said to have levered that flagstone up, found a stash of gold and sold it to the Manchester dealer Oliphant's, getting £3 10s (equivalent to around £450 today) for each gold piece.

In the late nineteenth century, it became fashionable among the wealthy to create a final resting place fit for a King. Aristocratic families began to design and commission tombs as grand as those built for Egyptian royalty. Imposing stone monuments featuring hieroglyphics and stone guardians including sphinxes, crocodiles and eagles began to appear all over Britain. The designs were often sizable in their construction but simplistic in design and shape. Egyptian-style tombs could endure the damp British weather and last through centuries, so their inhabitants would become famous posthumously, simply for their elaborate mausoleums.

The first-ever pyramid thought to have been built for funerary purposes in Britain can be found in the town of Nether Wallop, Hampshire. Standing at just over 15 feet high, next to the church of St Andrews, it was built for the physician Dr Francis Douce, ten years before he passed away aged 75 in 1760. Douce was morbidly obsessed with his own death, and he appointed the architect, John Blake, to design his pyramid-shaped tomb. Inspired by Ancient Egypt, Douce had read many books on early civilisation and was equally interested in the science of embalming bodies. Douce's imposing monument is complete with a carved-stone flaming torch, said to symbolise immortality. The tomb, which features the family crest on one side, is also rumoured to have been purposefully placed along meridian lines, often called ley-lines, which are said to be points of high magnetic energy linked to the spiritual realm and possibly alien lifeforms. The pyramid sits on top of a small mound and can be clearly seen in online images of the church. Douce left strict instructions in his will for the tomb to be maintained and left enough money to the parish minister for its upkeep for many years.

There is a pyramid in St John the Baptist's Churchyard in Pinner which a has novel addition to its design that became an ingenious resolution to an inheritance issue. Designed by the architectural writer, John Claudius Loudon, for his parents, the pyramid has a carved stone coffin thrust directly through its centre. This unique feature served a bizarre purpose: Loudon's parents had been named in a will by a wealthy benefactor some years before, but the will stipulated that both William and Agnes Loudon would continue to receive regular sums of money from the deceased's estate, as long as their bodies remained above the ground. The curious design of the pyramid, meant that Loudon would go on receiving the payments long after his parents' death. Local historians, however, believe that both parents were actually buried in a vault below the pyramid, and the stone coffin was simply a ruse to continue claiming the money.

Not all the pyramids found in British cemeteries were built to commemorate humans. A sparkling white pyramid set on Farley Mount, one of the highest points in Hampshire, marks the final resting place of a heroic horse named 'Beware Chalk Pit'. The horse belonged to Sir Paulet St John who was, at various times, a Member of parliament, Mayor of Winchester, and a keen fox hunter. A plaque on the front of the monument bears the legend:

> Underneath lies buried a horse, the property of Paulet St John Esq, that in the month of September 1733 leaped into a chalk pit twenty-five feet deep a foxhunting with his master on his back and in October 1734 he won the Hunters Plate on Worthy Downs and was rode by his owner and was entered in the name of Beware Chalk Pit.

Sir Paulet St John, was no doubt grateful to his horse for both saving his life and winning him a handsome sum of money at the races. A pyramid of this size would not have come cheap. The monument is described as a folly and, in archive photos, it seems to be exactly so. Nonetheless, the body of the horse — thought to be a chestnut-coloured mount — is certainly interred there. After being celebrated, along with his rider owner, in an 1840 publication of *Sporting Magazine* the horse became known as *Beware Chalk Pit* but was originally named *Fox-hunter*.

Another unusual horse burial is found in the village of Leckhampton, Gloucestershire. Several large blocks of Cotswold stone have been crudely placed in a pyramid formation, and a plaque marks the final resting place of the horse known as *The Continental*, who died in 1902, during a race at Cheltenham. The horse belonged to Henry Cecil Elews, owner of Colesborne Park, who erected the monument shortly after the horse's death. The spot has since become a popular picnic site as it sits high on a grassy knoll overlooking the vast rolling Cotswold hills.

The gardens of Blickling Hall in Norfolk are home to an impressive pyramid tomb. Standing at an incredible 45 feet (13.7 metres) high, the tomb contains the bodies of John Hobart, the Second Earl of Buckingham, who died in 1793, his first wife Mary Ann, and his second wife Caroline. The monument was designed by Joseph Bonomi the Elder, the same architect who designed Hannah Cortoy's tomb in London's Brompton Cemetery. Commissioned by the Earl's daughter, the ambitious tomb boasts a marble pavement and three carved stone sarcophagi, which were so heavy they had to be transported by water from London.

It was such a grand design that the daughter and her husband paid the equivalent of over £200,000 in today's money, and they were forced to sell jewellery to meet the bills. Bonomi was interested in ancient Egypt, and his son later became a celebrated Egyptologist. The Earl had also read a little of the early Egyptians, and he would have known that their tombs were designed to guide their occupants into the afterlife. Did he ask his daughter to build a monument impressive enough to honour the gods and secure a place in the hereafter for her parents? It is possible, but we shall never know for certain.

Another wealthy man obsessed with ancient Egypt was Charles Piazzi Smyth (1819-1900) an Italian-born British professor of astronomy who, along with his wife Jessica, became known for his meteorological and pyramidological studies. His parents travelled from Naples and settled in Bedford where they commissioned an observatory, in which Charles received his first lessons in stargazing. Developing an interest in ancient Egypt, Charles became convinced that the secrets of the universe lay deep in the Great Pyramid of Giza.

He travelled to Egypt several times and studied every angle of the Great Pyramid, taking photos and making sketches of its interior and exterior, many of which are still used by scholars today. Consumed by the idea that the pyramids were the product of divine intervention, his book attracted both praise and ridicule in his lifetime. Piazzi-Smyth designed his own funerary monument, based on the Great Pyramid, which can be found in St Johns Churchyard in Sharow, Yorkshire. Despite a lifetime of controversy regarding his work, Piazzi-Smyth is today considered to have played an important role in the history of astronomy and is famed for being Scotland's most prominent astronomer. Buried under the base of the pyramid with his wife, affectionately remembered on her memorial plaque as Jessie, Charles's somewhat lengthy epitaph states:

> *Astronomer Royal for Scotland from 1845 to 1888, who earned unperishing renown by his journeys to distant lands for scientific objects, and by his eminent Astronomical and other Scientific Writings and Researches. As bold in enterprise as he was Resolute in demanding a proper measure of public*

sympathy and support for Astronomy in Scotland. He was not less a living emblem of pious patience under Troubles and Afflictions, and he has sunk to rest, laden with well-earned Scientific Honours, a Bright Star in the Firmament of Ardent Explorers of the Works of their Creator.

The Egyptian styles, symbols and artifacts uncovered on expeditions from Napoleon Bonaparte's to Howard Carter's, have driven interest in Egyptology for centuries. The ostentatiousness of the death tombs of the Pharos undoubtedly struck a chord with the Victorians who were, anyway, fascinated by death. The many pyramids around the country — albeit miniature versions of those in Egypt — have not only stood the test of time under constant exposure to the British weather, but have united many in their hopes, desires, and fears of the afterlife.

Death for the ancient Egyptians was not the end but the beginning of a journey towards another world. When an Egyptian King or Queen was placed into a pyramid, their riches would be buried with them to ensure that they could continue to have wealth and familiar comforts with them in the next life. Even in today's secular world, that comforting idea has not entirely gone away.

Farley Mount marks the final resting place of a horse named 'Beware Chalk Pit'.

18 Honourable mentions

Not all funerary monuments mark the final resting place of a person or animal much loved by others in their lifetime. In my many journeys across Britain, I have also been able to view some of the most curious dolmans, ancient sacred stones and unidentified geological artifacts lurking in the shadows of graveyards and burial sites. They sit randomly on small mounds of earth or are found propped up against modern buildings, especially those built on former places of worship, or graveyards.

Many of Britain's churches were built on old foundations or the sites of pagan worship. Some of the monuments I have uncovered remind us of the old religions which were replaced by Christianity, or the later conflicts between Protestantism and Catholicism, depending on the monarch of the day.

The replacement of paganism by Christianity has meant that many ancient stones, dolmans, and carved symbols have been destroyed, leaving only a handful around the country. St Mary's Church on Cold Christmas Lane in Ware is a place often rumoured to have been used for devil worship. Nicknamed 'Cold Christmas Church', it often attracts pagans, modern witches, and satanists to its grounds, and on many of my visits to the church I have found scorched areas of grass where fires have been lit, pentagrams carved into the earth and unusual symbols sprayed on almost every wall.

However, despite its unnerving history, I found the church to be peaceful and inspiring. Set in a very rural part of Ware, it is alleged that the church received its nickname after dozens of local children froze to death during a very harsh winter many years ago and the bodies of the poor little mites are buried within the churchyard. The spirits of these children are believed by some to haunt the churchyard. Online ghost bloggers flock to the area to try and capture ghostly apparitions and video footage of anything unusual. Many have reported hearing the eerie moaning of children on night visits. I personally never experienced any moaning, but the church is surrounded by a large flock of sheep whose eyes light up in the dark and who bleat, a little like moaning children in the stillness of the night.

The church, which dates back to 1086, is in a state of disrepair and is deemed unsafe to enter. However, nestled away in the Hertfordshire countryside away from prying eyes, it is hard to deter would-be paranormal investigators or modern-day satanists. The church gets regular visits by those willing to risk the falling stones from the building. Paranormal experiences have been reported here for many years and the church is often documented as a 'go-see' for anyone interested in the spirit world.

One paranormal story from Cold Christmas Church allegedly happened in 1978, when a local woman was enjoying a walk on the grounds and is said to have encountered a whole platoon of soldiers who marched through the doorway of the church and passed right through her body without stopping. The story sounds fanciful, but it continues to attract visitors to the church. On one of my visits, however, I did experience a total loss of battery power on my phone. Having arrived with it fully charged, this seemed strange, especially when those with me experienced the same phenomenon, but when we got back to our cars the phones' batteries were mysteriously restored.

For all this, the church is a beautiful place, even if the effects of ramblers and the harsh British weather are sadly taking their toll on the building. I hope that the church stands for many centuries more or is restored as a working church and protected. I have always dreamed of converting a former church into a home for myself to live out my days. Cold Christmas Church would be ideal as long as Old Nick doesn't make an appearance of course.

In the corner of a car park in the Churchyard of St Mary the Virgin, Newington in Kent, sits a stone known as The Devils Stone. Believed to have once been part of two stones, it bears what looks like the imprint of a man's shoe. Local legend says that the Devil was infuriated by the constant ringing of the church bells and decided to steal them. He is said to have scaled the church spire, snatched up the bells, placed them in a sack which he slung over his shoulder, and then jumped from the belfry onto the two stones, wherein he left his fiery footprints. The shape on the remaining stone is more of a raised bump as opposed to an indentation but, nevertheless, it does resemble the shape of a man's shoe. It measures just over 38cm in length, making 'The Evil One' a British size five!

The second stone is believed to have been broken up in the 1930s and used as part of a wall within the church grounds. This was done following a lengthy argument between two councillors, both of whom died mysterious deaths shortly afterwards! According to the legend, the Devil ran off with the church bells but dopped them into a local stream as he fled. A wise old woman declared that the bells could only be retrieved by two pure white oxen. Two such beasts were found, and with the help of locals, they dragged the bells out of the water. However, when a local man called from the crowd that one ox had a black spot on its nose, the bells fell back into the water, never to be seen again. There is no date for the story, but the stone is formed from prehistoric mudstone and the grounds of the church may once been a neolithic burial chamber. Fossils and stones often contain shapes that resemble things that we are familiar with, but the shape on this particular stone does, undoubtedly, resemble a man's shoe.

Another stone that has a devilish story attached to it is the megalith that holds the record as Britain's largest standing stone. It resides, twenty-five feet tall, in The Church of All Saints, in the parish of Rudstone, East Riding in Yorkshire, and is estimated to weigh around forty tonnes. Composed of gritstone, local geologists have concluded that the stone must have been brought from a quarry located almost twenty miles away. Considering the possible age of the church, the placement of the stone suggests that early neolithic humans somehow transported it to the present site — also home to many ancient bones.

During an excavation of the church in the 1800s, experts found human remains close to the standing stone, and most of them seem to have been sacrificed. There is evidence of human sacrifice in many locations across Britain, usually predating the Roman occupation of these islands. The Romans also performed sacrificial offerings, but their ceremonies involved animals, not people. Research suggests that the stone may have been mostly embedded, almost to its top, until it was raised 5 feet during an excavation.

Sheela Na Gigs, are erotic, grotesque, and often crudely carved stones depicting figures flagrantly exposing their genitalia and can mostly be found on the tops, sides, and sometimes insides of churches and cathedrals. Most appear to be female, in a squatting position, and are almost always depicted exposing the vulva with both hands while smiling or grimacing. The exact beginnings of these unusual stones have baffled historians for years, but the carvings appear, in the main, to be from around the 11th or 12th century. They have been found in British and Irish Churches as well as French and Spanish buildings and places of worship. The female vagina is often perceived to be the portal to the world, and in many cultures, this female organ is considered to be a gateway between life and death. In some parts of Ireland, brides are encouraged to look at and seek blessings from a Sheela before weddings, to ensure that the bride will fall pregnant in due course.

Some scholars suggest that these unusual carvings may have been added to churches to ward off evil, as they are often seen positioned high above doorways or windows in places of worship. It is also possible that the carvings that survive are remnants of previous structures as many of our churches have been built on top of old ones. They may once have been a representation of mother nature, known as Gaia in paganism, which was replaced by Christianity around the sixth century in England.

Modern stone carvings were installed on Paisley Abbey in the early 1990s, delighting sci-fi fans when they discovered that a character from Ridley Scott's celebrated film *Alien* had been included. In 1991, Edinburgh-based stonemason David Lindsay and his team were commissioned to create 12 new gargoyles for the 13th-century abbey as almost all of the original ones had crumbled away. Gargoyles are intended to ward off evil spirits but they also channel water away from the walls of churches and buildings. Lindsay and a team of stonemasons created almost two dozen designs for consideration and just twelve made the cut for production. The new gargoyles raised little comment until 1997, when someone noticed that one of them closely resembled the character Xenomorph in Ridley Scott's film. Visitors now come to Paisley Abbey from all over the world just to see the gargoyle. The sandstone has begun to age and is now a grey colour, much like the rest of the building, so the new carving looks as though it has been sitting above an archway for centuries.

Lychstones are long slim stones which sit under lychgates: the porch-like structures, often with triangular rooves, which sit above the gates of churches. Lych is the old English word for corpse and these structures were installed in churches in the middle ages — before mortuaries became the norm — at a time when most people died at home. Coffins were placed on a bier (a moveable platform) and placed under the lychgate. The gates were often guarded by family members or clergy before a funeral could take place, to keep body snatchers at bay. The lychgate kept the rain off and there were seats placed around the inside of the gates for the watchmen to sit on and keep guard. Often, the first part of the funeral was conducted under the lychgate.

These gates also served to differentiate consecrated and un-consecrated ground. In English folklore, it is believed that the spirit of the last person to be buried stands under the lychgate to keep watch for the next person. From 1666 to 1814, parish priests were obliged to inspect a corpse to ensure that the body was correctly prepared for burial as there was a legal requirement for all corpses to be wrapped in a woollen shroud. The purpose of the rule was simply to protect Britain's then vital wool trade, but in poorer parts of the country the rule was often ignored.

The Little Chapel, or Shell Church is situated in Les Vauxbelets Valley, in the village of St Andrews. This wonderful shell and pottery-covered building was completed in 1914 by Brother Déodat, who wanted to create a miniature version of the grotto and basilica at Lourdes, the Rosary Basilica. The current structure is thought to be Deodat's third attempt: the first drew criticism from his fellow brothers and the second building was deemed too small when the Bishop of Portsmouth found that he could not fit through the door. After the Bishop's visit, Déodat demolished the chapel and set about commissioning the build of the third and current version which measures just 16 feet by 9 feet. Sadly, Brother Déodat never got to witness the finished church as he died during a visit to France in 1939.

The chapel fell into disrepair during the two world wars but was lovingly restored in 1977 by a local charity and is currently thought to be Guernsey's top tourist attraction. When I visited it during filming for a documentary in 2014, I was astounded to see how truly tiny the church is. There are just eight seats, and you have to crouch into some parts, but it is beautifully designed with a working altar, steps, and stained-glass windows. There is a spire, stone crosses on the roof and every inch of the chapel has been covered with seashells and small pieces of pottery. Guernsey is steeped in folklore, particularly relating to the fairy folk and The Little Chapel is a perfect visit for anyone interested in stories of the fae or for little children who love fairy stories. Believed to be the smallest consecrated church in Europe, this minute place of worship is a sight to behold.

Liverpool Cathedral holds the record for Britain's biggest church and is the eighth largest place of worship in the world. Construction began in 1904 and took seventy-four years to complete. The gargantuan building towers over the city of Liverpool and visitors can enjoy unobscured panoramic views from the tower which stands a whopping 500 meters above sea level. Based on designs by Giles Gilbert Scott, the building stands 331 feet (101 m) high, and it is also one of the world's tallest non-spired church buildings. Designed to represent the resurrection of Christ, the building is undeniably an architectural masterpiece.

19 The final chapter

My journey around Britain's graveyards has led me to think deeply about my own mortality. When I first began writing this book, I had yet to experience the loss of someone very close to me. Ambling around a churchyard and respectfully studying the graves of much-loved humans, I didn't fully grasp the importance of a headstone to a family who've lost a loved one. *Grave Concerns* grew from my passion for gothic architecture, a fascination for the mysteries of the past and my enjoyment of quiet places of reflection — away from the hubbub of city life.

I love searching for the oldest grave in a cemetery and trying to read its weather-beaten, lichen-covered headstone. The graves of animals, pets or children can be incredibly sad, but also beautiful. Carvings of lambs, for example, often indicate the grave of an infant. My nephew Liam, who is just six years old, recently saw the graves of children in a local cemetery and innocently asked my brother, 'Babies don't die, do they Daddy?'

Explaining death to a young child is never an easy task but it is a challenge our family recently had to tackle. A few months after I had written about my beloved uncle Lee, in the first chapter of this book, he was diagnosed with terminal cancer. Aged just 50, his illness hit our family hard. At first, I didn't want to accept it or believe it could be possible to lose him. He was the youngest, second only to me on my mother's side, and had been the baby of the family for a long time. We were all in shock and I was in denial for many months.

On 1 March 2022, my sweet uncle Lee took his final breath at the Macmillan hospice in Poole. I was unable to be at his side at the end, but he passed with many of the family around him and loved ones had been visiting him for months. Until that moment, I had never experienced the psychical pain of losing someone. My whole body hurt to know that he had gone, despite being warned that he would likely live for just a handful of months after the diagnosis. I had spent many days video calling him, encouraging him to stay positive, but he knew the cancer had the upper hand. He was simply too weak to cope with chemotherapy and so, after a short but brutal four-month battle, I lost my beloved uncle that fateful day in March.

He and I had spoken frankly about death in the months after his diagnosis. He was incredibly brave during his illness, and it was easy to talk to him about his funeral and what might happen on the other side. I had begged him, in the weeks before he passed, to visit me from the spirit world — if he could find a way to come back. He laughed and said that he wasn't sure if that was possible, but that he would try. I was comforted by the idea that it might not be the end and, if I missed him enough, he might be able to return. It was a naïve thought, but one I clung to and still do.

Planning a funeral, and dividing up personal items, were all things that needed to be organised, but it was a fraught and painful process for everyone involved. In the weeks before his cremation, I was finally able to understand the importance of planning a funeral and creating a final send-off for a loved one. The headstones I had been intrigued by — the tombs I had taken snaps of and the fascinating epitaphs I had discovered — all had grown from the deep emotional pain of a family experiencing a loss similar to mine.

Planning a funeral helps to take a person's mind off what has happened, albeit for just a few moments a day. Choosing songs and poems for a service helps remind us of the things a person enjoyed when they were alive. Choosing clothing for a loved one to be dressed in for burial, or cremation, allows a family to ensure that their loved one looks smart for that all-important crossing to the other side. In fact, every part of the process helps us to heal when a person dies.

During lockdown, I was cast in a Regency dating TV show and had to quarantine for ten days in a hotel in York. Due to covid restrictions I was allowed just one precious hour during the day to take exercise, as long as I didn't meet anyone outside my 'bubble'. I chose to spend each day walking around York cemetery with my daughter, Ivy, who was housed with me for the duration of the filming. It was a quiet place for my research and a welcome break for Ivy, who was becoming bored with the hotel room's four walls. It was late September 2021, and my dear uncle Lee was still alive and blissfully unaware of what lay ahead.

As I wandered through the broken slabs and crumbling monuments, I questioned the point of it all. Why would anyone care about me in 100 years, when my grave was overgrown and my headstone weathered and worn, or reduced to a pile of rubble? I even questioned why a family would go to the trouble of commissioning a headstone at all. At that moment, it all seemed like a waste of time and money, but I was only thinking of myself. I had little idea of the pain that lay ahead with the loss of someone so dear to me. I nonchalantly walked around the vast grounds of the cemetery wondering if it was selfish of me to be buried in a plot that family members might feel obliged to visit. I couldn't bear to think of my daughter, Ivy, feeling forced to come to a graveyard every Mother's Day, Christmas day, or anniversary of my passing. Ivy, who was two at the time, was busy running freely around the grounds shouting 'die', a word she had recently picked up, for some unknown reason, but it now seemed strangely fitting for the location we were in. Nevertheless, a funeral was taking place in the church at the time, so I was mindful not to allow Ivy to wander too close to the grieving relatives.

Since the passing of my uncle, I now have a greater understanding of gravestones. My personal experience of loss has added to my respect for the final resting places of those whom I will continue to visit, whenever I am near a cemetery or graveyard. I will always find their monuments interesting, and the epitaphs left by loved ones deeply touching, but I now have a better understanding of them.

While large monuments are often seen as a sign of wealth or prominence in a community, it makes perfect sense to honour a loved one with as grand a monument as is affordable. The Taj Mahal is often referred to as the world's largest and most elaborate memorial. Commissioned in 1631 by the fifth Mughal Emperor Shah Jahan after the passing of his wife Mumtaz Mahal, it is often described as a teardrop on the cheek of time. The Taj Mahal is an architectural wonder that took over twenty-two years to complete. Built almost entirely out of white marble, it sparkles day and night from its setting in Agra, India.

Mumtaz Mahal was described as Emperor Shah Jahan's soul mate and — before she died giving birth to the couple's fourteenth child — it is believed that she made her husband commit to four promises. The first was that he was to build the great Taj, the second was that he should never marry again. The third promise Mumtaz extracted from her husband was that he would be kind to their children and the final promise was said to be that he should visit her tomb on the anniversary of her death. Unfortunately, when Jahan was succeeded by his son, Aurangzeb, he was placed under house arrest and forced to forfeit his final promise.

Every year, this gargantuan monument of love and devotion receives over eight million visitors. Many aren't aware of its history until they arrive at its grounds and are informed by local tour guides. The bodies of Emperor Shah Jahan and his beloved wife Mumtaz are kept in the mausoleum part of the building, but Mumtaz was only interred there in 1653 when the building was finally completed. Her body had been kept in a garden on the shore of the river Yamuna for over twenty-two years after her death.

Roughly 55 million people die each year across the world, and it isn't just Britain that is running out of space. Across the planet cemeteries are overcrowded, and fewer new ones are being created. In 2013, the BBC reported that almost 25 percent of local authorities responsible for the majority of cemeteries in England expected grounds under their management to be completely full by 2023. Visiting the grave of a loved one in a cemetery may, one day, become obsolete. Perhaps my next of kin won't have a realistic option of burying me or having a headstone to mark my final resting place.

A family in Wales recently decided to add a personal touch to their loved one's funeral when he passed away aged just 32, leaving his wife and family devastated. As an award-winning tattoo artist, Lee Clements had worked on the well-known TV show *Gavin and Stacy* as an on-set advisor. His expertise had been needed for the episode where the deadpan character 'Nessa', played by Ruth Jones, decides to become a tattooist. He was well respected within his field and the whole tattoo community was deeply shocked when he passed at such a young age. The father of three, who owned the Chimera tattoo parlour in Barry, South Wales, was known for tattooing some of Britain's best loved celebrities. He had previously worked with the Welsh Government to secure tighter restrictions on tattooing to ensure better hygiene and safety within the industry.

Funeral celebrant, Ceri-Lou Newman, wanted to give Lee a ceremony that his family would cherish and remember, so she suggested that they incorporate Lee's love of ink. His funeral took place on 22 January 2020 and, as family gathered around, Ceri-Lou arranged for mourners to spray jets of coloured ink onto the top of the coffin. The family were delighted to offer Lee one last link to his favourite art. The ceremony will never be forgotten, and the family were able to share Lee's beloved artwork one last time, together.

While standing at the graveside of my grandfather, watching the small wooden box containing my uncle Lee's ashes being lowered into the ground, it seemed as though just a few years had passed since I stood and watched my grandfather's coffin being lowered into the same plot. Lee was just 51 when he died and his father had passed at only 52, also from complications of cancer. The cemetery was quite empty back in 1991, when I attended my grandfather's funeral, but it was now tightly packed with graves. Some of the new headstones are those of children. Sun-faded teddy bears and balloons adorn the graves, and although it is deeply distressing see the headstones of babies and children, I took some comfort from the fact that my dear uncle Lee will spend eternity surrounded by little ones. Lee never married or had children himself, but he would have been a fantastic husband and an awesome father, just as he had been an amazing uncle.

Lee's death reminded me that honouring someone when they pass is as much about those who are left behind as those who have departed. The need for a quiet place of reflection to think about a passed loved one, or a place to visit and quietly talk to the person we have lost, offers comfort when grief takes hold. I have learned that grief is like a wave, it can hit you at any moment. Calmly going about the day, we can be suddenly interrupted by a flood of sadness that seemingly comes from nowhere. A song might play on the radio or in a shop and you are instantly taken back to a memory of a loved one, reopening the painful wounds that grief always brings.

Since my uncle's death, my mind has sometimes produced strange images when I least expected them. There have been a few occasions when I could have sworn that I had seen my uncle in a shop, walking down the road, or in a car passing down the street. The hope in your heart that a loved one has passed to a better place helps us find solace when healing from a death. Planning a day to remember them, reminiscing, and remembering the good times all helps in the painful process of grieving. An epitaph on a grave means that family members can set in stone a final message that will last until they meet again if there is, indeed, another dimension or spirit world.

Messages of prayer can help some family members find solace in the idea that they are sending a loved one on a journey of faith. Planning a prank for a funeral can break the dark cloud of grief and make loved ones laugh. Building a huge tomb can be a reminder to some of how a character was in their lifetime. Grief takes time to both rise and diminish. You may never get over losing a loved one, but there comes a day when things become a little easier to cope with.

Grief is deeply personal, and everyone will experience it differently. Those who grieve may also begin to question their faith, or view of the world. For others, the passing of a loved one may strengthen their faith by providing a new understanding of the meaning of life. Grief is an experience often shaped by society and culture. Each culture has its own set of beliefs and rituals for death and bereavement. These too can deeply affect how a person experiences and expresses grief.

Monuments, tombs, headstones, and funerals help a family to find closure after a love one's passing which, in turn, allows a person to accept what has occurred and move forward in life. A cemetery is a place you can visit by yourself: no phones, noisy people, or other distractions. The older I become the more regularly I seem to feel the need to find peace.

When I began to visit cemeteries regularly — before I realised that my many visits constituted a hobby — I had not grasped how similar my pleasure was to my father's excitement when he took us on family outings to St Mark's Cemetery in Talbot Woods, long before my grandfather and uncle were buried there. My dad often used to say, 'What I am now, so shall you be', although, as an obstinate child, I thought I knew better.

Having finally experienced profound grief myself, I will continue to honour the resting places of those who have left us and, unintentionally, given me so much.

Nicola Kelleher is an an author, actress and television presenter who lives in London with her family and two dogs. She has always been fascinated by the paranormal and has regularly appeared as both a presenter and contributor on television shows. In 2012 she presented a documentary, *Supernatural Guernsey*, combining her passion for history with her knowledge of the paranormal. She has also presented wildlife television shows for Animal Planet, on location in Africa.

As well as *Grave Concerns*, she is the author of *Very Practical Magic* (2019) a modern take on witchcraft.

Also from SunRise

Deny & Disavow
Distancing the Imperial Past in the Culture Wars
Alan Lester

When Sean Became James
Martin McNamara
The inside story of the Bond legend

See Jane Fly
Feminism in Aviation
PETER PIGOTT

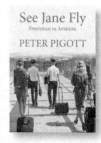

SOME PILO
NIGEL HARRISSON

The Golden Age of Flying Boats
Peter Pigott

Sky Talk
Stories from Flying's Golden Age
Philip Hogge

BOAC AND THE GOLDEN AGE OF FLYING
Britain's iconic global airline
Malcolm Turner

THE CONSTELLATIO
Lockheed's Graceful Masterpie
Alexander Clifton

IT'S PULL TO GO UP
From Lancasters to VC10s
A pilot's tale
Jeff Gray

Britain's Airline Entrepreneurs
From Laker to Branson
Malcolm Turner

Comets and Concordes
The pilot who flew the first and the fastest of all jet airliners
Peter Duffey

Ari, Jackie & Mar
The Pirate, The Princess & The
Onassis, Kennedy,
The Love Triang
the 20th Ce
Malcolm Tu

www.SunPub.info